THIS BOOK BELONGS TO:

CHRISTMAS 2004

Christmas
with Southern Living
2004

Christmas
with Southern Living®
2004

Edited by Rebecca Brennan and Julie Gunter

Oxmoor
House®

©2004 by Oxmoor House, Inc.
Book Division of Southern Progress Corporation
P. O. Box 2463, Birmingham, Alabama 35201

Southern Living® is a federally registered trademark belonging to
Southern Living, Inc.

ISBN: 0-8487-2752-5
ISSN: 0747-7791
Library of Congress Control Number: 2004105637
Printed in the United States of America
First Printing 2004

Editor in Chief: Nancy Fitzpatrick Wyatt
Executive Editor: Susan Carlisle Payne
Art Director: Cynthia Rose Cooper
Copy Chief: Allison Long Lowery

Christmas with Southern Living® 2004
Editor: Rebecca Brennan
Foods Editor: Julie Gunter
Assistant Foods Editor: Jane E. Gentry
Copy Editor: Donna Baldone
Contributing Copy Editors: Jacqueline Giovanelli, L. Amanda Owens
Editorial Assistant: Dawn Russell
Senior Designer: Melissa Jones Clark
Senior Photographer: Jim Bathie
Senior Photo Stylist: Kay E. Clarke
Photo Stylist: Ashley Wyatt
Illustrator: Kelly Davis
Director, Test Kitchens: Elizabeth Tyler Luckett
Assistant Director, Test Kitchens: Julie Christopher
Test Kitchens Staff: Kristi Carter, Nicole Lee Faber, Kathleen Royal Phillips,
    Jan A. Smith, Elise Weis, Kelley Wilton
Publishing Systems Administrator: Rick Tucker
Director of Production: Phillip Lee
Books Production Manager: Theresa L. Beste
Production Assistant: Faye Porter Bonner

Contributors
Copy Editor: Lauren Caswell Brooks
Indexer: Mary Ann Laurens
Interns: Amber Ballew, Julie Perno

Cover: Classic Roast Turkey and Gravy, pages 110–111; Cornbread Dressing Croquettes,
page 119; Cranberry-Orange Sauce, page 135
Back cover, clockwise from top left: Cracker Candy, pages 156–157, Chocolate Meringue
Cake, pages 148–149, European Holiday, pages 68–69, Featured Artist, page 47

To order additional publications, call 1-800-765-6400.

For more books to enrich your life, visit **oxmoorhouse.com**

contents

Easy & Elegant
Decorations

Have a seat and get ready to be transported into a wonderland of holiday decorations. These pages offer imaginative ways for you to express the spirit of Christmas throughout your home.

TRIMMINGS TO SUIT ALL TASTES

Whether you deck your halls in red and green or you prefer something less traditional, these pages will inspire you with fresh ways to decorate every room in your home with Christmas cheer.

◀ SET A PARTY MOOD

Wonderfully lush lengths of fabric trim this table and are a money-saving alternative to a tablecloth. Unfinished fabric edges are folded under. The buffet-style setup allows for an over-the-top centerpiece. For this arrangement, line the container with a plastic trash bag or other waterproof liner; then add water-soaked floral foam to help hold stems in place and keep them fresh. Place the longest stems first; then fill in with flowers and fruit, using floral picks for fruit.

SIMPLY STYLED ▲

Shiny pears, kumquats, lady apples, and greenery transform a hutch into a cozy decoration. A fresh arrangement in a copper container adds a burst of color to the shelf display. The leafy-design plates add interest behind the fruit and copper accents. In the south of France in the late 1700s, *santons*, or "little saints," were often placed at the Christmas crèche. Here, these collectible figures reflect that tradition and add height to the setting.

◀ NATURE'S GIFTS

A beautiful sleigh on a sideboard becomes more impressive when filled with natural materials. The deciduous holly, eucalyptus, seeded eucalyptus, and assorted greenery clippings used here will stay fresh for a week to 10 days when inserted into moistened floral foam. The apples, which are held in place with floral picks, may begin to soften sooner, depending on the room temperature.

LITTLE ACCENTS EVERYWHERE ▲

Use garlands and trims to dress every corner of your home for the season. An evergreen garland is cut into short lengths and used to adorn these handsome reindeer. Fresh flower sprigs are tucked in for color (floral water picks keep the blooms fresh). Also consider using garlands and greenery to trim picture frames, mirrors, chandeliers, and windowsills for a festive emphasis.

CREATE A SCENE

When the dining table is not being used for dining, make it a stage for dramatic decorations. A swath of fabric winds down the table, making a path for the metal reindeer. A large glass urn filled with coffee beans holds feathers, dried artichokes, and branches.

◀ COLOR MATCH

Plan your holiday color scheme to complement your sur-roundings. In this living room, the Christmas decorations echo the earthy tones of the walls and furnishings. The bronze and green ribbons that garland the tree, the coppery glint of the trees on the mantel, and the pheasant feather accents blend easily with the existing decor without sacri-ficing any festive ambience. Graceful boughs of greenery drape the mantel. Clusters of magnolia leaves add texture and give height where needed. The asymmetrical place-ment of the gilded trees makes an interesting frame for the arrangement, while the feathery wreath contributes warm tones and an appealing visual contrast to the trees.

FOREST SETTING ▼

When decorating for the season, consider any tabletop as the setting for a picturesque display. Here, a trio of pinecone trees easily conveys a holiday attitude. A few branches of pine and a couple of woolly felt ornaments are the only accents needed for a charming composition.

. . . make a topiary . . .

Topiaries are classic holiday decorations. These two versions, one fresh and fruity and one that can be used for years, are sure to become favorites.

FRESH FRUIT AND EVERGREENS

This evergreen tree is quite a showpiece due to its size and abundant garlands of fruit. You can make this topiary in a size to suit any setting. Here's how: Use a knife to shape blocks of floral foam into a triangular tree shape. Moisten the foam, and stack the blocks in a container lined with a waterproof bowl or plastic. Secure the blocks with long floral picks, and wrap the foam tree with chicken wire. Stick cuttings of greenery into the foam, entirely covering the shape. Use floral picks to secure rows of fruit to the tree. If your topiary is too small for a pineapple topper, use a cluster of greenery, small fruit, or ribbon instead.

FANCY FRINGED TREE

Eyelash fringe, purchased from a crafts store, gives a feathery frill to this little tree. To make the topiary, cover a plastic craft foam tree (ours is 18 inches tall) with eyelash fringe, using glue to hold it in place. Decorate the tree with miniature ornaments held in place with horseshoe-shaped pins or wire bent into U-shapes. Pin a bow to the top of the tree.

To display the topiary on a base, secure a block of plastic craft foam in a container that is the right size for the bottom of the tree. Glue fringe around the outside of the foam to hide the space between the foam and the container. Insert a dowel stick into the center of the foam base, then secure the topiary on the other end of the dowel stick.

...make it flowery...

Flowers signal a special occasion. Use them in unexpected places for eye-catching glamour. The rose wreath and luscious candle collars make this wooden hutch a featured attraction.

RING-OF-ROSES CHRISTMAS WREATH

Fashion a beautiful wreath of flowers for a fraction of what you would pay a florist. To begin, soak a floral foam wreath in water. (You can find the wreath forms at crafts and discount stores.) Allow the water to drain from the wreath form before adding fresh materials. Completely cover the wreath by sticking in stems of flowers. Roses were used for the wreath shown here; other options include carnations and kermit (chartreuse) mums. Add greenery accents, if desired.

FLORAL CANDLE COLLARS

Boost the candle power of ordinary pillars with fresh collars of blooms, berries, and greenery. Start with a candle adapter filled with floral foam that fits into the candleholder. (Candle adapters can be purchased at floral-supply stores, larger discount stores, and crafts stores. Precut rounds of floral foam, which are available at crafts and discount stores, can be substituted for the candle adapter. If you use floral foam, tape it crosswise with floral tape to the top of the candleholder to secure it.) Soak the foam in water. Drain it well before beginning. Push stems of greenery, berries, and flowers into the foam. Use a floral pick in the bottom of the candle, if necessary, to secure it to the foam base, making sure that the candle is tall enough so that the flame never meets the fresh materials.

Narodzenie Jezusa. Pasterze przy żłobku.

Narodjenje Isusovo.

COLLECTIVE CHARM
When it comes to arranging collections, there is strength in numbers. Here, nativity scenes are grouped on the top of a chest. To add impact to the grouping, small leaves, pieces of greenery, and hay serve as a base. Tiny potted conifers add height and create a backdrop. Votive candles fill in and contribute a warm glow.

CHEERFUL ACCENTS

Adding holiday highlights to your home doesn't have to take a lot of time or money, as this sunroom proves. Small wreaths in the windows, tiny wreaths on the birdhouses, gaily striped candles, and a dressed-up amaryllis give the space a festive face. To wrap the amaryllis stem, start at the bottom of the stem and crisscross with ribbon to the top. Tie a knot under the blooms.

. . . make a view . . .

*Windows are like frames just waiting to be
filled with a seasonal picture. Here are two ideas
that are easy to do and hard to top.*

◀ WINDOW DRESSING

Decorate your windows with containers full of color.
Shown here, a small metal container filled with greenery,
berries, and candy canes is held in place by a sheer ribbon
tacked to the window frame. Baskets and metal cones are
other options for this design.

ORNAMENTAL SPOTLIGHT ▼

A window provides a fitting frame to showcase special
ornaments. Use fishing line to suspend ornaments from
the window frame for an almost invisible hanger. Greenery
cuttings, berries, and pinecones wired together to form a
swag add an attractive finish.

FABULOUS FRONT DOORS

First impressions count, especially when it's your front door at Christmas. On these pages, we show seven of our favorites to spark your creativity.

CITRUS TWIST

A traditional front door treatment—a wreath and a garland—gets a fresh attitude. Lemon, lime, and kumquat embellishments on the wreath, pots of paperwhites and ornamental cabbages on the steps, and citrus-colored ribbons combine for a festive welcome. To attach fruit to the wreath, use floral picks that have wire at one end. Stick the pick into the fruit and wrap the wire around the wreath. The paperwhites fare better if kept inside on cold nights.

◀ FRESH OUTLOOK

This decoration uses a variety of greenery for maximum impact. A wicker cone on the screen door holds the abundant arrangement. Clippings from the backyard are ideal for this type of bouquet. To keep the cuttings fresh, place moistened floral foam in a plastic bag inside the container. Give each stem a new cut before sticking it into the foam to allow the stem to absorb moisture. Place long stems first, then fill in with a variety of greenery in shorter lengths. White twinkle lights and ribbon loops draw attention to the garland surrounding the door.

STACKED FOR STYLE ▲

For a wide door, you need a substantial wreath. The decoration pictured above is actually three separate wreaths—one small, one medium, and one large—that have been wired together to create a showier display. A seeded eucalyptus wreath is wired to the inside of a large evergreen wreath; then a small hypericum berry wreath is placed in the center and wired to the eucalyptus wreath. This technique creates a large wreath that has wonderful color and texture.

CASUAL ELEGANCE

A formal front entry gets a playful treatment thanks to long, winding vines twirling around the doorway. The look starts with evergreen trees in containers placed on either side of the door, which is framed by an evergreen garland. Citrus fruit accents the trees and the greenery-filled container hanging on the door. Kudzu vines tie all the pieces together and soften the traditional treatment. An oversize bow made from two different colors of ribbon is placed off center above the door for a graceful finishing touch.

▲ Greens for the Porch

Take advantage of a covered front porch to set a festive holiday scene. Lanterns surrounded by lacy branches of pine, spruce, and cedar add a charming welcome when arranged on a rustic table. Wreaths hanging by ribbons in the windows enhance the tabletop setting.

A Cheery Greeting ▶

A vintage Santa poster covers the front door and sets a merry tone. Garlands around the arched entry and door provide a good frame, while the large red bow above the door links all the red elements together. Big gift boxes and a tree of lights hint at the jolly old elf's Christmas Eve journey. If they aren't in a covered area, bring the gifts inside during rain or snow.

. . . make a wreath . . .

*A variety of looks are easy to create when
you start with a basic grapevine wreath.*

◄ BUILT TO LAST

Fashion a beautiful wreath that can be used
year after year from a vine wreath and an
assortment of dried florals. Purchase
unadorned grapevine wreaths and dried
materials at crafts and discount stores. To
make the wreath, stick stems of dried materials between the vines of a plain wreath.
Place larger materials first, then add the
smaller accents. Give the wreath a distinctive personality by placing lengths of vine
or thin branches around the outside. Use
wire to attach a ribbon bow.

CLASSIC RED AND GREEN ►

The Christmas standard is an evergreen
wreath trimmed with red ribbon. Make the
one pictured here by sticking evergreen
clippings into a plain grapevine wreath. A
variety of evergreens, such as pine, cedar,
spruce, and boxwood, makes a richly tex-
tured wreath; or use just one type of greenery for a more uniform look. Attach ribbon
loops and bows to the wreath with wire.

FESTIVE FOYERS

Wow visitors and family alike with an entryway that is decked out in holiday finery. The ideas on these pages, from a fluffy garland of fresh materials to a tree trimmed with Christmas cards, will inspire you to design a unique greeting of your own.

POINSETTIA HIGHLIGHTS

A luxurious mixed greenery garland is the star of the show in this foyer (facing page and above). The green branches contrast dramatically against the white banisters. Bonsai poinsettias (available at discount and garden stores) punctuate the garland with bright bursts of color. For this decoration, each tiny poinsettia was planted in a yogurt cup covered with moss. Pieces of wire—punched through the cup on three sides, then twisted together at the top and bent to form a hook—allow the cups to hang exactly where desired on the garland. Ribbons and white lights finish the design with finesse.

▲ BIG STYLE ON A SMALL SCALE

Make the most of decorations in a small entry by concentrating an arrangement in one area. Here, a side table is the setting for an extravaganza of flowers, fruit, and greenery. A large, moss-covered plastic craft foam ball, strategically placed in the center of the container, means fewer flowers and fresh materials are needed. Pillar candles surrounded by clusters of kermit mums make good design partners.

PRESENT PERFECT ▶

Placed in a decorative bowl, cleverly wrapped gifts are conveniently at hand to delight your holiday guests, and they make a top-notch decoration as well. Moss topiaries, ribbon-wrapped balls, and pottery containers give the vignette an earthy ambience. (For details on how to make the wrapping paper, see page 168.)

. . . make a personal greeting . . .

*Use favorite Christmas cards from the past and present for
a heartfelt decoration brimming with good wishes.*

CHRISTMAS CARD ORNAMENTS

Create a place of honor for Christmas cards whose holiday thoughts and good cheer become more precious with each passing year. Use a hole punch to make a hole in the top of each card. Thread a narrow ribbon through the hole to make a hanger. Ribbon embellished with a decorative element, such as the flower on the ribbon detailed below, adds a nice finish to the card. Hang the cards on the branches, and stand back to watch as this tree becomes the main attraction for all who come near.

A Fresh Look at Fireplaces

Second only to the tree, fireplaces are a main focus of holiday style. Gather 'round as we showcase several approaches suitable for a variety of moods.

FINE FLOURISHES

This look works equally well whether your fireplace is grand in scale or cozy
and casual. Tiny conifers planted in clay pots are trimmed with clear glass
beads that add frosty highlights (facing page and above). Lemon leaves
sprayed with silver paint adorn an evergreen wreath, and silver ornaments
dotted among the branches of a garland add sparkle. A bead garland is draped
along the mantel. Chandelier pendant-style ornaments add points of interest
to the garland and catch the twinkle of light from the nearby Christmas tree.

WOODLAND APPEAL
A pinecone candelabra is the centerpiece of a collection of old-world Santas. Twig trees, pinecones, and pine branches give a foresty feel to the setting. Let the colors in your room play a role in your selection of materials. Here, colors suggested by the painting are reflected in the candles, bead garland, and stockings.

◀ COLLECTIVE CHARM

Earth-toned colors and materials come together for a handsome fireplace scene. Note how the swoop of fabric gives visual weight to the garland and introduces a rich color to set off the rustic tones of the wise men, candle-holders, and angels. A pair of fur-trimmed stockings adds color to the front of the fireplace and leads the eye to the hearth arrangement, where twig trees, luminarias, and a bucket of kindling extend the decoration all the way to the floor.

FEATURED ARTIST ▲

Let a seasonal painting be the central focus on the mantel. A painting of Santa stars here, but a child's Christmas drawing offers an excellent alternative. Create splashes of color with candles and containers of flowers. Candy canes are a fun addition, too. A wreath is hung above the painting to add height to the arrangement.

. . . make it fresh . . .

*Chartreuse green reindeer moss and lady apples lend a whimsical mood to
tree-shaped topiaries and a playful garland. Maidenhair fern—not generally thought
of as a Christmas accent—is a perfect fit for this design.*

◀ REINDEER MOSS TREES

To make the topiary, attach moss to a plastic craft foam tree
using U-shaped floral pins or glue, completely covering the
tree. Insert a dowel or small stick into the bottom of the
tree, then insert the other end of the dowel into a container
filled with a block of plastic craft foam. Stack lady apples
on top of the container to cover the foam.

APPLE AND MOSS GARLAND ▶

Thread small lady apples on a sturdy wire, leaving a small
space between the apples. After threading the apples, alternately glue tufts of moss and sprigs of boxwood between
the apples.

◀ GARDEN-VARIETY GRANDEUR

A garden gate turned on its side sets the theme for this exuberant supersize decoration. To get this look, place an evergreen garland along the mantel. Position pots of amaryllis, maidenhair fern, ornamental cabbage, and ivy on the mantel. The pots will help hold the garland in place. Add pillar candles. If necessary, set the pots and candles on boxes or stacks of books to achieve the desired heights. Fill in around the pots with stems of greenery. Magnolia branches are a good choice because one branch fills a large area and helps conceal stems of other cuttings. A wreath hanging on the gate continues the design upward.

ENCHANTING EVERGREENS ▲

Potted conifers and amaryllis line up on this mantel. An evergreen garland hides the pots, and branches of deciduous holly offer spikes of color. The entire effect is multiplied by the reflection from the mirrors hanging above the mantel. A wreath hangs from a ribbon attached to the mirror frame. Achieve a similar look by resting the wreath on top of the mantel.

▲ ROYAL FOCUS

Three golden wise men are a striking decoration that need only a few additional accents. Beaded gold trees, tall candleholders, and jewel-toned ribbon play up the central focus of the mantel treatment. Wispy cuttings of greenery bring the various elements together.

MESSAGE ON A MANTEL ▶

Seasons greetings spelled out on a garland find a perfect setting between columns of the chimneypiece of this bedroom fireplace. The silvery tree on the hearth and slim silver vases filled with white lilies convey a winter wonderland feeling in the room.

OLD-WORLD INFLUENCE

A mix of accessories on this mantel—a rusty metal grill, wooden candleholders, richly colored ornaments, and a transferware tureen—lend this array a European ambience. Start the decorating process by gathering favorite things from your cabinets and shelves. Fancy stockings secured by faux evergreen tree holders are a fun, eye-catching highlight.

. . . make a candle stand . . .

A small tree trunk and a basic saw turn out candle bases that are simply wonderful.

WOOD BLOCK CANDLEHOLDERS

Create a uniquely charming base for pillar candles by cutting a small tree trunk or branch into sections. You may choose to visit the local Christmas tree lot and collect the trunk sections from the trimmed trees (be sure to protect surfaces from tree sap). These little wood blocks work well with woodsy companion pieces and can be equally appealing arranged down the center of a dining table. If desired, place a glass hurricane globe over each candle and stand.

DECORATING WITH FRUIT

Fruit as a decorating material has everything going for it—it's fresh, fragrant, easy to find, and inexpensive. The following pages show a lot of ways to make fruit the star of your holiday decorations.

FRUIT EXTRAVAGANZA

This splendid sideboard design shows the many ways you can use fruit to decorate for the holidays (facing page and above). Pineapples surrounded by apples and kumquats take the place of pillar candles on stately iron candleholders. Smaller candleholders contain a pomegranate and a grape-and-pear combination, while cranberries embellish a taper and fill a glass candleholder. A delicate garland, made by stringing fresh cranberries on thin floral wire, swirls around and down the sides of the mirror. Tendrils of ribbon provide a luminous effect. For the centerpiece of the arrangement (above), large hurricane vases hold pillars surrounded by cranberries, apples, grapes, and kumquats.

▲ Flowery Accents

A tiered metal stand is a good choice for a colorful display of fruit. For a similar look, stack footed cake stands or compotes. Pears, lady apples, and pomegranates are placed around clay pots filled with pansies. A pot of rosemary at the top gives the setup a tree shape. The style of this arrangement works well as a festive touch on a buffet or on a dessert or coffee bar for an open house.

Seasonal Still Life ▶

This serene grouping is the best kind of holiday arrangement. It's easy to assemble, stays fresh for at least a week, and can be used as a centerpiece, sideboard, or coffee table decoration. Plus, you can move it from kitchen to dining room to living room, as desired. The basic ingredients are a wide, shallow bowl; pillar candles; and fruit. Elevate the candles on small boxes or small bowls, as needed, and fill in with fruit.

LEMON LEAF AND CITRUS GARLAND

This lemon leaf garland offers a refreshing change of pace from the traditional evergreen variety (facing page and above). Bouquets of lemons and limes with bright red deciduous holly stems fill in among the leaves. Wide ribbon weaves down the length of the garland. The fruit is held in place by floral picks that have wire at one end. The pick is inserted into the fruit, and the wire is wrapped around the garland. Holly berries are inserted snugly into the garland. If wire-edge ribbon is used, it can be folded into a loop and tucked into the garland; however, floral wire can be used to hold it in place, if necessary.

. . . make a pretty lemon tree . . .

*This cheery little tree adds a bright accent wherever it's placed, whether it's used
as a breakfast table centerpiece or used in multiples along a mantel or dining room table.*

A TREE OF LEMONS AND ROSES

In addition to being beautiful, this boxwood tree
adorned with lemons and roses will stay fresh
for at least a week. To make the tree, use a knife to
trim floral foam blocks into a tree-shaped
triangle. Moisten the floral foam, then use floral
picks to hold the blocks together. (Wrapping
the shape with chicken wire will help hold the
shape.) Place the tree form on a plate to protect
the tabletop from moisture.

Completely cover the tree form with sprigs of
boxwood. Use floral picks to attach the fruit. Stick
stems of roses into the foam. Fold lengths of ribbon
into loops and tuck them among the foliage. Place
oranges around the base of the tree, if desired.

FRUIT TREE ▶

Escape the ordinary and opt for a fruit-filled tree this Christmas. Here, a mix of
fresh and faux fruits blends together for a tasteful display. To make a hanger for
the apples, stick a thin floral wire up through the bottom of the apple, then
bend the wire and push it back through from the top, leaving a small loop at
the top of the fruit. Twist the wire ends together at the bottom of the apple.
Thread a ribbon through the loop and tie the ends to form a hanger. Fill in
among the branches with ribbon loops.

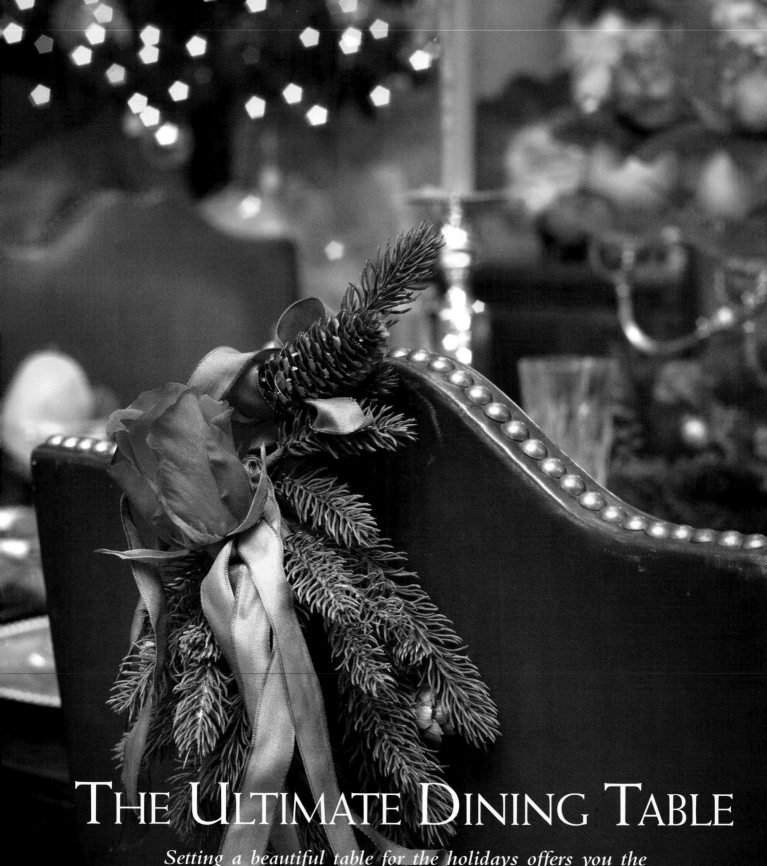

THE ULTIMATE DINING TABLE

*Setting a beautiful table for the holidays offers you the
opportunity to express an inviting welcome to family and friends.
Take a look at the dozens of ideas on these pages, then let
your imagination be your guide.*

FORMAL FARE

Adorn your dining room chairs with a fresh accent (facing page) and then go all out to set a dressy mood on the table (above). For the chairs, wire together a single rose (in a floral water vial), greenery, pinecones, and ribbons. For the table, pull out your crystal and silver, and get creative with nuts, fruits, and flowers. Here, an evergreen wreath encircles the base of a silver epergne that holds a bouquet of roses. Oranges placed on the epergne's "arms" hold rosebuds whose stems are wired to floral picks and stuck into the fruit.

▲ THE HEIGHT OF GOOD DESIGN

Raising the centerpiece from the surface of the table gives the piece more presence and also keeps the arrangement out of the way. A wooden stand is a good base for the copper container filled with fruit, flowers, and berries that offer a rich complement to the china and glassware. Woven chargers are used in lieu of place mats or a tablecloth.

ABOVE AND BEYOND THE TABLE ▶

Here's a fine example of coordinating the table setting with the room decorations. Fruit embellishments dress the chandelier and the wreaths that hang in the window. For the hanging fruit, insert floral wire in the bottom of the fruit, bend it slightly and push back through the fruit, leaving a small loop at the top. Twist the wire ends together at the bottom of the fruit. Hang with ribbon.

EUROPEAN HOLIDAY

This quaint setting exudes a charmingly festive ambience. A classic French country pattern on the seat covers and chandelier shades pairs with a toile tablecloth and burlap topper. Table linens, dinnerware, and glasses provide red and gold highlights. The rooster candelabra centerpiece is surrounded by a wreath of evergreens, berries, and flowers. Red beeswax candles add a bright finishing touch.

To make a burlap topper, cut a square of burlap. Burlap comes in a 72-inch width, so no seam is necessary. Measure where you would like the fringe to start, and pull out the innermost thread first; then work from the outside in.

◀ ROOM AT THE TOP

A lightweight garland draped on the arms of a chandelier is the hands-down winner as the quickest, easiest decoration with the most dramatic punch. On this chandelier, a pinecone and seed garland interweaves with a garland of glass leaves and berries for a beautiful complement to the table setting.

◀ A FORESTY SCENE

For a style that's casual and woodsy, set your table with a rustic centerpiece surrounded by pine cuttings, beaded ornaments, pinecones, and berries. On this dining table, a grand reindeer with a rusty patina is the center of attention. Tiny sprigs of pine are tucked around pinecone candles that sit atop the wooden candleholders and in the reindeer's antlers. Table runners turned horizontally on the dining table act as place mats.

HUNG WITH CARE ▶

Christmas stockings make terrific chair decorations. With an abundance of stockings available, you can choose virtually any look you want to coordinate with your table setting. This oak leaf design stocking matches the table runner shown at left. Fill stockings with greenery, berries, toys, small wrapped packages, or candy canes, and tie them to chairs with ribbon.

. . . make a favor . . .

The thrill of getting a party favor is something we never outgrow. Here are a few treats you can make that are guaranteed to be well received.

PLACE CARD WREATH ▶

Glue tiny pinecones to a miniature grapevine wreath for a tasteful place card and chair decoration. Paint it gold, if you like, or leave it natural for a casual appearance.

To make the place card, cut heavy paper to fit behind the wreath. Write the name on the paper, and glue it to the back of the wreath, leaving a space at the top open for the ribbon. Thread a ribbon between the paper and the wreath, and knot the ribbon around the chair. After the party, the wreath can be used as an ornament.

◀ SHEER DELIGHT

A translucent drawstring bag holds a special ornament as a memento of a festive meal. These little bags can be purchased at crafts stores. With the addition of a paper tag, they work well at the dining table as a combination place card/place favor. They are also a good way to present small gifts—and, as an added benefit, they can be used again and again.

BUTTON-TRIM DESIGNS ▷

Add holiday style to plain cocktail napkins by sewing on tiny buttons in seasonal shapes. On the napkins shown here, green buttons and an ivory star button form a miniature tree. Santa, snowman, and angel buttons, as well as other Christmas motifs, can be found at crafts stores. Use these to add a cheery accent to napkins or guest towels. These trimmed treasures make excellent party favors or hostess gifts.

◁ A WELCOMING GLOW

Invite guests to their seats with the shimmering light of a votive candle nestled among shiny pebbles. A dessert cup serves as the candle-holder. Tie a ribbon around the stem of the cup, and attach a name tag to the ribbon.

Look for inexpensive dessert cups or dishes at yard sales or discount stores. It's not necessary for the cups to match. Decorative pebbles can be purchased at crafts and discount stores.

▲ SO EASY, SO CUTE

A colorful mix of ribbons and the sparkle of ornaments help brighten dark wood. Lengths of red gingham and light green ribbons tie shiny red ornaments to the backs of these dining chairs, including them in the overall decorating scheme.

VISIONS OF SUGARPLUMS ▶

A stocking stuffed with goodies is a delight to behold whether you're 8 or 80! So put that marvelous vision to work as a highlight of the holiday trimmings. Hang a stocking or two in the window, and fill in around them with wreaths, garlands, gingerbread men cookies, or ornaments.

◀ CHRISTMAS WONDERLAND

Layer it on for a wondrous holiday setting. Lots of festive trimmings come together around this dining table to transform the room. Fun polka-dot plates and mugs get the whimsical theme started, and the sprightly Santa statue surrounded by a candy wreath completes the look. To make the candy wreath, see pages 76–77.

. . . make it fun . . .

Set a table that exudes joyous good cheer. A lively candy wreath and creative cutlery
that can be painted in minutes are two charming ways to get the festive look going.

◄ COLORFUL CUTLERY

Custom-design fun flatware just for Christmas. Start with a set of knives, spoons, and forks that have plastic handles. Wash and dry the flatware. Following manufacturer's directions, brush the handles with surface conditioner, and allow them to dry. Paint designs on the handles, as desired. After the paint has dried, brush the handles with one to two coats of clear glaze. Wait a week to 10 days before using or washing the flatware. Handwashing is recommended. (We used Perm Enamel surface conditioner, paint, and satin glaze for tile, glass, and ceramic.)

◄ CANDY WREATH

To make the candy wreath, spray paint a plastic craft foam wreath red or green. Hot-glue an assortment of candies to the wreath. Lollipops and candy canes don't require gluing—just stick them into the wreath. For the wreath shown here, miniature cupcakes were attached with floral picks inserted into the wreath and then into the bottoms of the cupcakes.

This wreath will last all season and for many years to come. Before storing it, remove the cupcakes, then place the wreath in a large plastic bag.

◄ NATURAL FOCUS

A tidy carpet of moss creates a stage for rustically elegant urns and square pots. Berried branches of deciduous holly, pillar candles, a bead garland, and table linens provide rich red accents. Plastic craft foam fills in the urns and pots. Moss, which can be purchased in bags at crafts and discount stores, covers the tops of the containers. The holly sticks easily into the foam; the candles sit on top of it.

For maximum impact, think beyond the table when decorating the dining room. Here, a collection of silver pieces on the mantel reflects the sparkle from the candles. Surrounded by greenery and a bead garland, and joined by bold stockings held by holders spelling out Noel, the arrangement is a handsome counterpart to the table.

. . . make it glow . . .

Moss is an inexpensive material that takes on a surprisingly festive attitude with just a few embellishments. These candleholders are a fitting decoration, whether on the dining table, sideboard, or mantel.

CORDING AND MOSS CANDLEHOLDERS

To make a candleholder, wrap a terra-cotta pot with sheet moss. Glue the moss to the pot to hold it in place. Wind cording, twine, or ribbon around the moss-covered pots. Place a pillar candle in the top, and tuck moss around the candle to conceal the opening. Sheet moss and pots can be purchased at crafts and discount stores.

▲ AGLITTER WITH GOLD

Sheer and shimmery, a simple-to-make table runner and seat covers dress the dining room in sophisticated yet comfortable style. Sparkling ornaments placed atop glass candleholders take the place of tapers. Ribbons tied through the hanging loops add a fitting finish. The ornate party favors double as napkin holders.

To make the table runner, sew a border of complementary fabric around a rectangular length of fabric. Turn unfinished edges under and stitch in place.

DINNER DRESS ▶

Use a lightweight fabric to design a glamorous detail for your dining chairs. Lay a tape measure across the seat of each chair to determine the dimensions you want for the seat cover. Cut a rectangle of fabric to these dimensions. Turn unfinished edges under and stitch in place.

Lay the fabric over the seat and gather it around each side of the chair back. Pin the fabric to the seat or use tiny Velcro dots with adhesive backing to hold the fabric in place. Tie cording and tassels around the sides of the chair, as desired.

Season's Best Recipes

What's your fancy this holiday season? Whether it's bar cookies to excite children and adults alike, herbs for savory or sweet palates, or classics from appetizers to desserts, you'll delight in stirring up these tried-and-true favorites.

OUR BEST BAR COOKIES

Caramel-Nut Bar Cookies

CARAMEL-NUT BAR COOKIES

Chewy and crunchy, and sweet and salty line up perfectly in these decadent bars. These cookies are for the more advanced baker.

½ cup butter, softened
¼ cup powdered sugar
1 teaspoon vanilla extract
1 cup all-purpose flour
1¼ cups granulated sugar
1 cup heavy whipping cream, divided
1 cup butter, cut into 16 pieces
1¼ cups coarsely chopped assorted nuts, toasted
   (we tested with pecans, natural almonds, and lightly
   salted macadamia nuts)
6 (1-ounce) semisweet chocolate squares, finely
   chopped

Beat ½ cup butter at medium speed with an electric mixer until creamy. Gradually add powdered sugar, beating well. Add vanilla; beat well. Gradually add flour, beating at low speed until blended.

With floured fingertips, press dough into a lightly greased 8" square pan. Bake at 325° for 25 minutes or until golden brown. Let cool on a wire rack.

Place granulated sugar in a medium-size heavy skillet. Cook, stirring constantly, over medium heat 8 minutes or until sugar is caramel-colored. (Sugar will become crumbly before caramelizing.) Reduce heat to low; gradually add ⅔ cup whipping cream, stirring to combine. (Mixture will sputter.) Add 1 cup butter, 4 pieces at a time, stirring until smooth after each addition (about 7 minutes). Remove caramel from heat; let cool 10 minutes.

Sprinkle nuts over baked crust. Pour caramel over nuts. Cool completely.

Place remaining ⅓ cup whipping cream in a microwave-safe glass measuring cup. Microwave at HIGH 1 minute or until hot. Pour hot cream over chopped chocolate in a bowl. Let stand 2 minutes. Whisk until smooth. Pour chocolate over cooled caramel, spreading chocolate to edges. Cover and refrigerate until layers are firm. Keep refrigerated until ready to serve. Let stand 5 minutes at room temperature before cutting and removing bars from pan. Yield: 20 bar cookies.

FUDGY PEPPERMINT BROWNIES

Who says "bar" cookies have to be rectangular? For a fun presentation, cut these ultrarich brownies with a 2" round cutter. The scraps make great nibbling.

1 cup butter or margarine
4 (1-ounce) unsweetened chocolate squares
4 large eggs
2 cups sugar
1½ cups all-purpose flour
½ teaspoon salt
1 tablespoon vanilla extract
1 teaspoon peppermint extract
½ cup coarsely crushed hard peppermint candies
   (about 20)
2 teaspoons powdered sugar

Melt butter and chocolate in a heavy saucepan over medium-low heat, stirring until smooth; let cool.

Beat eggs at medium speed with an electric mixer 2 minutes; gradually add 2 cups sugar, beating well. Add melted chocolate, flour, and next 3 ingredients; beat well. Stir in peppermint candy. Pour batter into a greased and floured 13" x 9" pan.

Bake at 350° for 32 to 33 minutes. Cool completely on a wire rack. Cut into bars; sprinkle with powdered sugar. Yield: 2 dozen.

Fudgy Peppermint Brownies

Peanut Brittle Blondies

make ahead • gift idea

HOLIDAY CANDY FUDGE BARS

Red and green candies dot these luscious bars with Christmas color.

2   cups uncooked quick-cooking oats
1½ cups all-purpose flour
1   cup chopped pecans
1   cup firmly packed light brown sugar
1   teaspoon baking soda
¼   teaspoon salt
1   cup butter or margarine, melted
1½ cups red and green candy-coated chocolate pieces, divided
1   (14-ounce) can sweetened condensed milk

Combine first 6 ingredients, stirring well. Add butter, and stir or beat at low speed with an electric mixer until mixture is crumbly. Reserve 1½ cups crumb mixture; press remaining crumb mixture into a lightly greased 13" x 9" pan. Bake at 375° for 10 minutes. Cool on a wire rack. Reduce oven temperature to 350°.

Place 1 cup chocolate pieces in a microwave-safe bowl; microwave at HIGH 1 to 1½ minutes, stirring after 30 seconds. Press chocolate pieces with the back of a spoon to mash them. (The candies will almost be melted with pieces of color coating still visible.) Stir in condensed milk. Spread mixture evenly over crust in pan, leaving a ½" border on all sides.

Combine reserved 1½ cups crumb mixture and remaining ½ cup chocolate pieces; sprinkle evenly over chocolate mixture, and press lightly.

Bake at 350° for 25 to 28 minutes or until golden; cool in pan on wire rack. Cut into bars. Yield: 3 dozen.

editor's favorite • gift idea

PEANUT BRITTLE BLONDIES

Dress up classic blonde brownies with peanut brittle from your local candy shop. They're big, rich bars—easy to stack and pack for holiday giving.

1½ cups firmly packed light brown sugar
¾   cup butter
2   large eggs
2½ cups all-purpose flour
2½ teaspoons baking powder
½   teaspoon salt
3   cups coarsely crushed peanut brittle (about 14 ounces)
2   teaspoons vanilla extract

Combine brown sugar and butter in a saucepan over medium heat; cook until butter is melted. Remove from heat. Cool slightly; add eggs, 1 at a time, beating until blended after each addition. Combine flour, baking powder, and salt in a bowl; stir into brown sugar mixture. Stir in peanut brittle and vanilla. Press dough into a greased and floured 13" x 9" baking dish.

Bake at 350° for 25 minutes or until golden. Cool in pan on a wire rack. Cut into bars. Yield: 2 dozen.

Holiday Candy Fudge Bars

Caffe-Cream Cheese Brownies

make ahead
CAFFE-CREAM CHEESE BROWNIES

With subtle coffee flavor, these dark-swirled brownies will please even noncoffee drinkers.

4   (1-ounce) unsweetened chocolate baking squares
4   (1-ounce) semisweet chocolate baking squares
⅓   cup butter or margarine
1½ tablespoons instant coffee granules
2   tablespoons hot water
2   (3-ounce) packages cream cheese, softened
¼   cup butter or margarine, softened
2   cups sugar, divided
6   large eggs
1   teaspoon vanilla extract
2   tablespoons all-purpose flour
1½ cups semisweet chocolate morsels,
       divided
2   teaspoons vanilla extract
1   cup all-purpose flour
1   teaspoon baking powder
1   teaspoon salt

Melt first 3 ingredients in a small saucepan over medium-low heat, stirring occasionally. Cool.

Stir coffee granules into hot water until dissolved. Cool.

Beat cream cheese and ¼ cup butter at medium speed with an electric mixer until creamy; gradually add ½ cup sugar, beating well. Add 2 eggs, 1 at a time, beating until blended. Stir in coffee and 1 teaspoon vanilla. Fold in 2 tablespoons flour and ½ cup chocolate morsels; set batter aside.

Beat remaining 4 eggs in a large bowl at medium speed; gradually add remaining 1½ cups sugar, beating well. Add melted chocolate mixture and 2 teaspoons vanilla; beat well. Combine 1 cup flour, baking powder, and salt; fold into chocolate batter. Stir in remaining 1 cup chocolate morsels.

Spread half of chocolate batter evenly in a greased 13" x 9" pan. Pour cream cheese batter over chocolate batter. Top with remaining chocolate batter; swirl with a knife.

Bake at 325° for 45 minutes (wooden pick will not come out clean). Cool completely in pan on a wire rack. Cut into squares. Yield: 2½ dozen.

Note: Line your pan with aluminum foil to ensure pretty squares and easy cleanup.

COCONUT-RASPBERRY LINZER BARS

Reminiscent of the traditional linzertorte, these convenient bars flaunt a tropical coconut flair.

1½ cups all-purpose flour
1   cup slivered almonds
½   cup sweetened flaked coconut
¼   cup sugar
½   teaspoon ground cinnamon
½   teaspoon grated lemon rind
¼   teaspoon salt
¼   teaspoon ground cloves
¾   cup cold butter, cut into pieces
2   egg yolks
1   cup seedless raspberry jam
Garnish: powdered sugar

Process first 8 ingredients in a food processor until almonds are finely ground. Add butter; pulse 10 times or until crumbly. Add egg yolks; process 15 seconds or until dough forms a ball. Set aside one-third of dough. Press remaining dough in bottom and ½" up sides of a lightly greased 11" x 7" baking dish. Spread jam to edges of dough.

Roll out remaining dough to ¼" thickness. Cut dough into ½" wide strips; carefully arrange strips over jam in a lattice design.

Bake at 325° for 37 minutes or until golden. Cool completely on a wire rack; cut into bars. Garnish, if desired. Yield: 15 bars.

HOLIDAY HERBS

Herb and Cheese Coins

HERB AND CHEESE COINS

Walnuts and blue cheese blend deliciously in these little savory cookies. Pour your favorite wine, and welcome your friends over.

2   (4-ounce) packages crumbled blue cheese, softened
½   cup butter, softened
1⅓ cups all-purpose flour
⅓   cup toasted, ground walnuts
1   egg white, beaten
Tiny fresh herb sprigs (we tested with rosemary, thyme, and sage)

Beat cheese and butter at medium speed with an electric mixer until creamy. Add flour and nuts; beat until blended.

Shape dough into 2 (8") logs. Wrap logs in wax paper, and chill 2 hours or until firm. Cut into ¼"-thick slices, and place on lightly greased baking sheets. Brush lightly with beaten egg white. Press herb sprigs firmly into each slice.

Bake at 350° for 12 to 15 minutes or until golden. Cool 1 minute on baking sheets; remove to wire racks to cool completely. Yield: 4 dozen.

Make-Ahead Tip: You can chill logs of dough overnight, and slice and bake the next day.

HERBED NUTS

Turn these nuts into a toasty snack with just a few minutes of baking and some fresh herbs. Serve them when guests come for dinner.

2   cups pecan halves
2   cups cashews
⅓   cup butter, melted
2   tablespoons minced fresh rosemary
1   tablespoon chopped fresh thyme
1   teaspoon salt
½   teaspoon ground sage
½   teaspoon ground red pepper

Combine all ingredients in a large bowl; stir well. Spread nuts on an ungreased jellyroll pan. Bake at 350° for 20 to 25 minutes, stirring every 10 minutes. Cool completely in pan. Store in an airtight container. Yield: 4½ cups.

ROSEMARY BUTTERMILK BISCUITS

These buttery biscuits pair nicely with ham for a holiday buffet (photo on page 93).

2   cups self-rising flour
1   tablespoon chopped fresh rosemary
⅓   cup cold butter, cut into pieces
¾   cup buttermilk
2   tablespoons shortening
2   tablespoons butter or margarine, melted

Combine flour and rosemary. Cut ⅓ cup butter into flour mixture with a pastry blender until crumbly; add buttermilk, stirring until dry ingredients are moistened.

Turn dough out onto a lightly floured surface; knead 3 or 4 times. (Don't overwork the dough.)

Place shortening in a 10" cast-iron skillet. Place skillet in 450° oven for 5 minutes.

Meanwhile, pat or roll dough to ½" thickness; cut with a 2½" round cutter, and place biscuits in hot skillet.

Brush biscuits with 2 tablespoons melted butter. Bake at 450° for 14 minutes or until tops are golden. Yield: 6 biscuits.

Note: If you don't have a cast-iron skillet, biscuits bake perfectly on an ungreased baking sheet at 450°, omitting the shortening.

Herbed Nuts

PARKER HOUSE HERB LOAVES

Parker House rolls snuggled together on a baking sheet bake into a single loaf you won't even need a knife to serve. Just break off individual rolls from these herb loaves, and tuck a sliver of ham or turkey inside.

4   cups bread flour, divided
2   (¼-ounce) envelopes rapid-rise yeast
2   tablespoons sugar
1   tablespoon garlic salt
1¼ cups milk
⅓   cup butter
2   large eggs, lightly beaten
½   cup butter, softened
2   tablespoons chopped fresh oregano
2   tablespoons chopped fresh basil
2   tablespoons minced onion
Garnish: fresh thyme

Combine 1 cup flour, yeast, sugar, and garlic salt in a large mixing bowl; stir well.

Combine milk and ⅓ cup butter in a saucepan; cook over medium-low heat until mixture reaches 120° to 130°, stirring often.

Gradually add hot milk mixture to flour mixture, stirring well. Add eggs; beat at low speed with an electric mixer until blended. Beat 2 minutes at medium speed. Gradually stir in enough remaining flour to make a soft dough.

Turn dough out onto a well-floured surface, and knead until smooth and elastic (about 6 to 8 minutes). Shape into a ball. Place in a well-greased bowl, turning to grease top. Cover and let rise in a warm place (85°), free from drafts, 30 minutes or until doubled in bulk.

Meanwhile, combine ½ cup softened butter, herbs, and onion; stir well. Set aside.

Punch dough down; turn out onto a lightly floured surface, and knead lightly 4 or 5 times. Divide dough in half. Roll half of dough to ¼" thickness; cut with a 4" round cutter.

Spread 2 teaspoons herb butter on tops of dough rounds; fold in half, bringing bottom within ¼" of top half, allowing herb butter to peak through top. Place half-moons upright next to each other on a greased baking sheet.

Repeat procedure with remaining dough and herb butter, making a second loaf. Cover and let rise in a warm place, free from drafts, 20 minutes or until doubled in bulk.

Bake at 375° for 14 minutes or until lightly browned. Brush loaves with remaining herb butter. Garnish, if desired. Yield: 2 loaves.

CRUSTY FRENCH PISTOU BREAD

Use a single-edged razor blade in firm, decisive strokes to slash the tops of these round loaves without deflating the rise.

3½ to 4½ cups bread flour
2   (¼-ounce) envelopes rapid-rise yeast
1   tablespoon sugar
1½ teaspoons salt
⅓   cup olive oil
½   cup minced fresh parsley
1   cup chopped fresh basil
1   cup grated Parmesan cheese
4   garlic cloves, minced
1⅓ cups warm water (120° to 130°)
1   tablespoon cornmeal
1   large egg, lightly beaten
1   tablespoon water

Combine 3½ cups flour and next 3 ingredients in a large bowl; add oil and next 4 ingredients. Stir until blended.

Add warm water; blend well. Turn dough out onto a lightly floured surface, and knead until smooth and elastic (about 5 to 10 minutes), adding remaining flour as needed.

Place dough in a well-greased bowl, turning to grease top. Cover and let rise in a warm place (85°), free from drafts, 45 minutes or until doubled in bulk. Punch dough down; turn out onto a lightly floured surface, and knead lightly 4 or 5 times. Divide dough in half. Shape each portion into a round loaf, and place on a lightly greased baking sheet sprinkled with cornmeal. Cut slashes into top of each loaf, using a sharp razor blade or knife.

Combine egg and 1 tablespoon water, stirring well; gently brush egg wash over loaves. Cover and let rise in a warm place, free from drafts, 20 to 25 minutes or until doubled in bulk.

Place a shallow pan on lower oven rack; fill with boiling water. Place loaves on rack above.

Bake at 400° for 20 to 25 minutes or until loaves sound hollow when tapped. Remove from pan immediately, and cool completely on wire racks. Yield: 2 loaves.

Crusty French Pistou Bread,
Rosemary Buttermilk Biscuits (page 91),
Parker House Herb Loaf

Herbed Sugar Cookies

editor's favorite • make ahead

HERBED SUGAR COOKIES

Rosemary and thyme make a surprisingly delightful appearance in these classic sugar cookies.

1   cup butter, softened
1¼ cups sugar
1   large egg
2⅔ cups all-purpose flour
½   teaspoon salt
2   tablespoons chopped fresh thyme
2   tablespoons chopped fresh rosemary

Beat butter at medium speed with an electric mixer until creamy. Gradually add sugar, beating well. Add egg; beat well. Stir together flour and salt; add to butter mixture, beating at low speed until blended. Stir in herbs.

Divide dough into fourths. Roll each portion to a ¼" thickness on a lightly floured surface. Cut dough with assorted Christmas tree cookie cutters. (We used cutters ranging from 1½" to 5½" in size.) Place on ungreased baking sheets.

Bake at 350° for 8 to 10 minutes or until very lightly browned. Let cool 1 minute on baking sheets. Remove to wire racks to cool completely. Yield: 3 to 4 dozen.

Note: Because size of cookie cutters can affect baking time, check cookies often while in the oven.

make ahead

WHITE CHOCOLATE-THYME TRUFFLES

Use these intriguing candies as place card holders on your holiday table. (See photo below.)

6   tablespoons whipping cream
3   (4-ounce) packages white chocolate baking bars, finely chopped (we tested with Ghirardelli)
2   tablespoons unsalted butter
4   teaspoons grapefruit rind
1   (1-pound) package vanilla bark coating
1½ tablespoons fresh thyme leaves (do not chop)

Bring whipping cream to a simmer in a small heavy saucepan over medium heat. Remove from heat; add white chocolate, butter, and grapefruit rind, stirring until smooth. Pour white chocolate mixture into a small metal bowl; cover and chill 2 to 3 hours or until firm.

Shape white chocolate mixture into 1¼" balls (about 1 tablespoon); cover and chill truffles 8 hours or until firm.

Melt vanilla bark according to package directions. Cool. Dip truffles in coating; place on wax paper. Sprinkle with thyme leaves while coating is wet. Let stand until firm. Store truffles in refrigerator. Yield: 2½ dozen.

. . . truffle tips . . .

• Use good quality white chocolate for truffle making. You'll taste the difference.
• Citrus and fresh herbs are a nice flavor pairing. To get fine grapefruit rind, use a Microplane™ grater.
• Fresh thyme leaves look festive sprinkled onto these candies. To remove leaves easily, just strip them from the woody stem (no chopping needed).
• Use a cookie scoop to shape truffle balls evenly.

ROSEMARY ROASTED TURKEY

Our golden turkey is rubbed with rosemary butter beneath the skin, giving the plump breast meat a burst of fresh herb flavor.

1 (¾-ounce) package fresh rosemary sprigs, divided
¼ cup butter, softened
Grated rind from 1 large lemon (2 teaspoons)
1 (15- to 18-pound) bone-in turkey
3 tablespoons salt
1½ tablespoons paprika
1 tablespoon pepper
11 garlic cloves, crushed
2 lemons, quartered
2 onions, cut into wedges
¼ cup butter, melted
2 cups dry white wine
1 cup orange juice

Chop enough rosemary to equal 2 tablespoons; set aside remaining rosemary. Combine chopped rosemary, ¼ cup softened butter, and lemon rind in a small bowl; stir well.

Remove and discard giblets and neck from turkey. Rinse turkey with cold water; pat dry. Loosen skin from turkey breast without detaching it.

Carefully rub rosemary butter under skin.

Combine salt, paprika, and pepper; sprinkle turkey inside and out with seasonings. Place 7 garlic cloves and lemon quarters in body and neck cavities; stuff with onion wedges and all but 2 remaining rosemary sprigs.

Tucking wingtips under, place turkey, breast side up, in a large shallow greased roasting pan. Tie ends of legs together with string.

Bake, uncovered, at 325° for 30 minutes. Baste with melted butter; bake 30 more minutes.

Combine remaining 4 garlic cloves, 2 reserved rosemary sprigs, wine, and orange juice; pour into roasting pan.

Bake, uncovered, 3 more hours or until a meat thermometer inserted into thigh registers 180°, basting with pan juices every 30 minutes. If necessary, cover turkey loosely with aluminum foil to prevent overbrowning.

Transfer turkey to a serving platter. Cover with foil, and let stand 20 minutes before carving. Skim fat from pan drippings, and serve drippings with turkey. Yield: 15 to 18 servings.

gift idea

SUGARED ROSEMARY BRANCHES

Not intended to be eaten, use these sugared branches to garnish a pumpkin pie, fruitcake, or other holiday cake, or to decorate a gift package or embellish a centerpiece. You can prepare this recipe with small rosemary sprigs that come in bunches at the grocery store, but the effect won't be as dramatic as with long branches from a winter garden.

6 (8" to 10") fresh rosemary branches
2 egg whites, lightly beaten
2 cups superfine sugar

Using a small pastry brush, brush 1 rosemary branch with egg white (do not dip branches into egg white). Working over a wire rack and wax paper, sprinkle rosemary heavily with sugar through a wire-mesh sieve, turning to coat. Shake off excess sugar; place rosemary on wire rack to dry. Repeat with remaining rosemary, egg white, and sugar. Let rosemary stand at least 8 hours or until dry; use immediately, or keep up to 1 week, uncovered, at room temperature. Yield: 6 decorative herb branches.

Tip: Make your own superfine sugar by pulsing granulated sugar in a food processor for about 30 seconds.

SOUTHERN LIVING
CHRISTMAS CLASSICS

Elegant Pumpkin-Walnut
Layered Pie (page 103)

CITRUS BATIDA

Let guests man the blender for this festive beverage with Caribbean flair. Just premeasure ingredients into one-batch containers, and chill.

2   cups orange juice
2   cups Ruby Red grapefruit juice
⅔   cup fresh lemon juice
¾   cup superfine sugar
1   cup rum

Process all ingredients in a blender until frothy. Serve over crushed ice. Yield: 5 cups.

—*Marvin Woods*
Hollywood, Florida

POINSETTIA PUNCH

Chill the champagne and juice in the refrigerator before the party; then mix the punch right before serving.

1   (750-milliliter) bottle Champagne, chilled
3   cups cranberry-apple juice drink, chilled
¼   cup thawed frozen white grape juice concentrate
¼   cup orange liqueur

Citrus Batida,
Poinsettia Punch

Stir together all ingredients in a 2-quart pitcher.
Serve in Champagne flutes. (Decorate serving tray with fresh cranberries, if desired.) Yield: 8 cups.

Nonalcoholic Punch: Substitute 1 (750-milliliter) bottle nonalcoholic champagne (such as Champagne Inglenook) for the Champagne, and ¼ cup orange juice for the orange liqueur. Yield: 8 cups.

—*Ginger Owings*
Memphis, Tennessee

PESTO TORTE

12   slices provolone cheese (about 12 ounces)
1   (8-ounce) package shredded mozzarella cheese
1   (8-ounce) package cream cheese, softened
1   (3-ounce) package cream cheese, softened
1   (8-ounce) jar dried tomatoes in oil, undrained (we tested with L'Esprit)
1   (7.5-ounce) jar pesto in olive oil (we tested with Bellino)
¼   cup mayonnaise
2   tablespoons unsalted butter, softened
¼   teaspoon garlic powder
¼   teaspoon pepper
Garnishes: pesto, fresh basil leaves, dried tomatoes

Line an 8" x 4" or a 9" x 5" loafpan with plastic wrap, allowing 5 to 6 inches to hang over edges; coat plastic wrap with vegetable cooking spray. Line bottom and sides of pan with provolone cheese slices, overlapping cheese slices to completely cover pan.

Process mozzarella cheese and next 8 ingredients in a food processor or blender until smooth, stopping to scrape down sides.

Spoon cheese mixture into prepared pan, pressing with spatula. Fold excess cheese and plastic wrap over torte; chill 12 hours.

Invert chilled torte onto a serving dish; discard plastic wrap. Serve torte with assorted crackers. Garnish, if desired. Yield: 12 to 14 appetizer servings.

—*Myrt Haas*
Bay St. Louis, Mississippi

Olive Tea Sandwiches,
Spicy Monterey Jack
Cheese Logs

make ahead
OLIVE TEA SANDWICHES

1   (7-ounce) jar pimiento-stuffed olives, drained and
    chopped
½   small onion, diced
2   hard-cooked eggs, chopped
1   cup chopped pecans, toasted
1   cup reduced-fat mayonnaise
2½ (16-ounce) loaves white bread slices (about 50
    slices), toasted (we tested with Pepperidge Farm
    Sandwich Bread)

Stir together first 5 ingredients. Cover and chill at
least 1 hour.

Spread 1 heaping tablespoon olive filling on 1 side of
25 bread slices; top with remaining bread slices. Trim
crusts from sandwiches; cut each into triangles, or cut
with round cookie cutters. Yield: 4 dozen triangles.

—*Linda Metzger*
Lumberton, North Carolina

make ahead
SPICY MONTEREY JACK CHEESE LOGS

A pair of these savory spreads makes a great holiday gift.

1   (8-ounce) package cream cheese, softened
1   teaspoon Worcestershire sauce
¼   teaspoon ground red pepper
1   (10-ounce) block extra-sharp Cheddar cheese, shredded
1   (8-ounce) block Monterey Jack cheese with peppers,
    shredded
1   cup chopped pecans or walnuts, toasted
½   cup chopped fresh parsley
Garnish: fresh parsley sprigs

Combine first 3 ingredients in a large bowl; blend well.
Stir in shredded cheeses. Divide cheese mixture in half,
and shape each portion into an 8" log.

Combine pecans and chopped parsley; roll logs in nut mixture. Cover and chill 8 hours. Let stand 1 hour before serving.
Serve with crackers. Garnish, if desired. Yield: 2 (8") logs.

Make-Ahead Tip: Wrap each log in heavy-duty plastic
wrap, and freeze. Thaw in refrigerator overnight.

—*Charles Flournoy*
Dallas, Texas

make ahead
HICKORY-SMOKED BOURBON TURKEY

1   (11-pound) frozen whole turkey, thawed
2   cups maple syrup
1   cup bourbon
1   tablespoon pickling spice
Hickory wood chunks
1   large carrot, scraped
1   celery rib
1   medium onion, peeled and halved
1   lemon
1   tablespoon salt
2   teaspoons pepper
Garnishes: grapes, pears, cranberries, persimmons,
    pomegranates, kumquats

Remove giblets and neck from turkey; reserve for
other uses, if desired. Rinse turkey thoroughly with cold
water, and pat dry.

Add water to a large stockpot, filling half full; stir in
maple syrup, bourbon, and pickling spice. Add turkey
and, if needed, additional water to cover. Cover and chill
turkey 2 days.

Hickory-Smoked Bourbon Turkey

Soak hickory wood chunks in fresh water at least 1 hour. Prepare charcoal fire in smoker; let fire burn 20 to 30 minutes.

Remove turkey from water, discarding water mixture; pat turkey dry. Cut carrot and celery in half crosswise. Stuff cavity with carrot, celery, and onion. Pierce lemon with a fork several times; place in neck cavity.

Combine salt and pepper; rub seasonings over turkey. Fold wings under, and tie legs together with string, if desired.

Drain wood chunks, and place on coals. Place water pan in smoker, and add water to depth of fill line. Place turkey in center of lower food rack; cover with smoker lid.

Cook 6 hours or until a meat thermometer inserted into thickest portion of turkey thigh registers 180°, adding additional water, charcoal, and wood chunks as needed. Remove turkey from smoker, and let stand 15 minutes before slicing. Garnish, if desired. Yield: 12 to 14 servings.

—*Chuck Behnke*
Peachtree City, Georgia

SWEET ONION PUDDING

This recipe brings out the best of the South's sweet onions by caramelizing and baking them in a creamy custard.

½	cup butter or margarine
6	medium-size sweet onions (3¼ pounds), thinly sliced and separated into rings
2	cups whipping cream
1	(3-ounce) package shredded Parmesan cheese (¾ cup plus 2 tablespoons)
6	large eggs, lightly beaten
3	tablespoons all-purpose flour
2	tablespoons sugar
2	teaspoons baking powder
1	teaspoon salt

Melt butter in a large skillet over medium heat; add onion. Cook, stirring often, about 45 minutes or until onion is caramel-colored. Remove from heat.

Meanwhile, stir together cream, cheese, and eggs in a large bowl. Combine flour and next 3 ingredients; gradually stir into egg mixture.

Stir onion into egg mixture; spoon into a lightly greased 11" x 7" baking dish. Bake, uncovered, at 350° for 30 to 32 minutes or until slightly firm, puffed, and golden. Yield: 8 servings.

—*Jan Moon*
Birmingham, Alabama

BRAISED CHESTNUTS

2	tablespoons butter or margarine
1	medium onion, finely chopped
1	cup dry red wine or port
3	cups chicken broth
1	pound whole chestnuts, shelled (about 3 cups nut meat)
1	tablespoon chopped fresh thyme
⅛	teaspoon salt
¼	teaspoon pepper

Melt butter in a Dutch oven over medium heat; add onion, and sauté 10 minutes or until tender and slightly browned. Add wine, and bring to a boil; cook, stirring occasionally, 1 minute.

Add broth and remaining ingredients; reduce heat to medium-low, cover, and simmer 1 hour or until chestnuts are tender and liquid is almost absorbed. Yield: 6 servings.

Note: You can buy a jar of already shelled chestnuts at Williams-Sonoma.

—*Nancy and Gary Petitt*
Townsend, Delaware

BRUSSELS SPROUTS WITH APPLES

Crisp, sweet apples and crunchy water chestnuts complement tender Brussels sprouts in this seasonal side dish.

2¼	pounds fresh Brussels sprouts
3	tablespoons fresh lemon juice
2½	teaspoons salt, divided
¼	cup butter or margarine, divided
1	medium onion, diced
¼	cup apple juice
1	apple, diced (we tested with Braeburn)
1	garlic clove, minced
1	teaspoon sugar
1	(8-ounce) can sliced water chestnuts, drained
½	cup golden raisins
2	teaspoons grated lemon rind
½	teaspoon freshly ground pepper
⅛	teaspoon ground nutmeg

Rinse Brussels sprouts; remove discolored leaves. Cut off stem ends, and cut each in half lengthwise. Place Brussels sprouts, lemon juice, 1½ teaspoons salt, and water to cover in a large saucepan. Bring to a boil; reduce heat, and simmer 8 to 10 minutes or until tender. Drain. Set Brussels sprouts aside; keep warm.

Melt 2 tablespoons butter in a large skillet over medium-high heat; add onion, and sauté 15 minutes or until onion is browned and tender, stirring often. Add apple juice; cook 2 minutes, stirring to loosen browned particles.

Add apple, garlic, and sugar; cook, stirring constantly, 5 to 6 minutes or until apple is tender. Add water chestnuts, next 4 ingredients, remaining 1 teaspoon salt, and remaining 2 tablespoons butter; cook, stirring constantly, 3 to 4 minutes. Stir in Brussels sprouts. Yield: 8 to 10 servings.

—*Mary Ann Lee*
Marco Island, Florida

editor's favorite • quick & easy

CRISPY PEANUT BUTTER-CHOCOLATE TREATS

Kids will love these familiar crisp cereal bars gone chocolate and made into lollipops.

1½ cups sugar
1½ cups light corn syrup
1½ cups chunky peanut butter
6   cups crisp rice cereal
2   cups semisweet chocolate morsels

Cook first 3 ingredients in a large saucepan over medium-low heat, stirring constantly, until blended and mixture begins to bubble. Remove from heat.

Combine cereal and chocolate morsels in a large bowl. Stir in hot peanut butter mixture until combined. Spread mixture into a 13" x 9" pan lined with plastic wrap. Cool completely. Lift out of pan. Cut into stars or other shapes, using 2" cookie cutters, or cut into squares. Yield: 22 stars or 16 squares.

Note: To make lollipops, insert 4" paper craft sticks into cutouts.

Crispy Peanut Butter-Chocolate Treats

Grandmom Lucy's Orange Crispies, Nutcracker Sweets

GRANDMOM LUCY'S ORANGE CRISPIES

Andrew Cochran got this recipe for these family favorites from his grandmother, Lucy Cochran.

1   cup shortening
1   cup sugar
1   large egg
1½ teaspoons orange extract
1¾ cups all-purpose flour
½   teaspoon salt

Beat shortening at medium speed with an electric mixer until creamy. Gradually add sugar, beating until light and fluffy. Add egg and orange extract, beating well.

Combine flour and salt; add to shortening mixture, beating until blended.

Drop dough by rounded measuring teaspoonfuls, 2" apart, onto ungreased baking sheets.

Bake at 375° for 11 to 12 minutes or until edges are lightly browned. Cool 1 minute on baking sheets; remove to wire racks, and cool completely. Yield: 3 dozen.

—*Andrew Cochran*
Blue Ridge, Virginia

NUTCRACKER SWEETS

These will remind you of wedding cookies with cherries.

1   cup butter, softened
¼   cup granulated sugar
½   teaspoon almond extract
2   cups all-purpose flour
1½ cups ground almonds
¼   teaspoon salt
1   (6-ounce) jar maraschino cherries, drained and
    chopped
Powdered sugar

Beat butter at medium speed with an electric mixer until creamy; gradually add ¼ cup granulated sugar, beating well. Add almond extract, beating well.

Combine flour, almonds, and salt; add to butter mixture, beating well. Pat cherries between paper towels to remove excess moisture; stir cherries into dough.

Shape dough into 1" balls. Place 1" apart on ungreased baking sheets.

Bake at 325° for 16 to 18 minutes or until bottoms are lightly browned. Cool 2 minutes on baking sheets.

Roll cookies in powdered sugar twice. Transfer cookies to wire racks to cool completely. Yield: 4 dozen.

—*Teddy Grieger*
Oceanside, California

GRANNY'S CHRISTMAS COOKIES

Dress up these Christmas cookies by dipping the bottom of each baked cookie into melted chocolate. Let chocolate harden before serving.

2   cups butter or margarine, softened
1   cup sugar
2   large eggs
2   egg yolks
2   teaspoons vanilla extract
4¼ cups all-purpose flour
⅛   teaspoon salt
1   cup red and green candied cherries, halved

Beat butter at medium speed with an electric mixer until creamy. Gradually add sugar, beating until light and fluffy. Add eggs and egg yolks, 1 at a time, beating until blended after each addition. Stir in vanilla.

Combine flour and salt; add to butter mixture, beating just until blended. Cover and chill dough 1 hour.

Shape dough into 1" balls. Place 2" apart on lightly greased baking sheets. Press a candied cherry half into center of each cookie.

Bake at 350° for 20 minutes or until edges are lightly browned. Cool 1 minute on baking sheets; remove to wire racks, and cool completely. Yield: 5 dozen.

—*Ann Bostick*
Temple, Texas

CRUNCHY ALMOND COOKIES

For a chewy almond cookie, bake only 25 minutes.

1   pound slivered almonds
2   cups powdered sugar
2   teaspoons vanilla extract
2   egg whites
Coarse sugar

Process almonds in 2 batches in a food processor 1 minute or until finely ground. Stir together almonds, powdered sugar, and vanilla in a medium bowl, using hands to mix. Stir in egg whites. (Dough will be sticky.)

Shape dough into 1" balls; dip tops in coarse sugar, and place on lightly greased baking sheets.

Bake at 325° for 30 minutes. Cool 1 minute on baking sheets. Remove to wire racks to cool completely. Yield: about 5 dozen.

editor's favorite

ELEGANT PUMPKIN-WALNUT LAYERED PIE

A pecan pielike filling nestles beneath the creamy pumpkin topping (photo on page 96).

1   (15-ounce) package refrigerated piecrusts
1   large egg, lightly beaten
1¼ cups firmly packed light brown sugar, divided
1   cup chopped walnuts, toasted
3   tablespoons butter, melted
¼   teaspoon vanilla extract
1   (8-ounce) package cream cheese, softened
2   large eggs
1   (15-ounce) can pumpkin
2   tablespoons all-purpose flour
1   teaspoon ground cinnamon
½   teaspoon ground ginger
½   teaspoon ground allspice
½   teaspoon ground nutmeg
Whipped cream (optional)

Roll 1 piecrust to press out fold lines; cut out pastry leaves, using a 2" leaf-shaped cookie cutter. Brush leaves with beaten egg. Place leaves on an ungreased baking sheet. Bake at 425° for 6 to 7 minutes or until golden. Cool completely on a wire rack.

Fit remaining piecrust into a 9" pieplate according to package directions; fold edges under, and crimp. Bake at 425° for 6 minutes.

Combine ½ cup brown sugar and next 3 ingredients; spread in bottom of baked piecrust.

Beat cream cheese at medium speed with an electric mixer until creamy. Gradually add remaining ¾ cup brown sugar, beating well. Add eggs and pumpkin, beating well.

Combine flour and next 4 ingredients; add to cream cheese mixture, beating until blended. Pour cream cheese filling over walnut layer.

Bake at 425° for 10 minutes. Reduce oven temperature to 350°, and bake 30 more minutes or until pie is set; remove from oven. Cool on wire rack. Arrange pastry leaves on pie. Serve warm or chilled with whipped cream, if desired. Yield: 10 servings.

—*Gloria Bradley*
Naperville, Illinois

Mystery Pecan Pie

editor's favorite

MYSTERY PECAN PIE

Taste pecan pie and cheesecake together in this decadent dessert.

1   (15-ounce) package refrigerated piecrusts
1   (8-ounce) package cream cheese, softened
4   large eggs
¾   cup sugar, divided
2   teaspoons vanilla extract, divided
¼   teaspoon salt
1   cup chopped pecans
1   cup light corn syrup
2   tablespoons butter, melted

Unfold and stack 2 piecrusts; gently roll or press together. Fit into a 9" pieplate according to package directions; fold edges under, and crimp.

Beat cream cheese, 1 egg, ½ cup sugar, 1 teaspoon vanilla, and salt at medium speed with an electric mixer until smooth. Pour into piecrust. Sprinkle with pecans.

Stir together corn syrup, melted butter, remaining 3 eggs, remaining ¼ cup sugar, and remaining 1 teaspoon vanilla; pour mixture over pecans.

Bake at 350° for 50 to 55 minutes or until set. Cool completely. Yield: 8 servings.

—*Gretchen Eickhorst*
St. Charles, Missouri

SWEET POTATO CRÈME BRÛLÉE

A French specialty gets a Southern accent with a layer of sweet potato.

1   large sweet potato, baked, skinned, and mashed
¼   cup firmly packed light brown sugar
1   tablespoon fresh lemon juice
2   cups whipping cream
¾   cup granulated sugar
7   egg yolks, lightly beaten
1   tablespoon vanilla extract
⅓   cup firmly packed light brown sugar

Combine mashed sweet potato (about 1¼ cups), ¼ cup brown sugar, and lemon juice; spoon potato mixture into a buttered 10" x 2" quiche dish to form a ¼" thick layer.

Stir together cream, granulated sugar, egg yolks, and vanilla in a medium saucepan. Cook mixture over medium-low heat, stirring constantly, about 15 minutes or until hot. (Do not boil.)

Pour over sweet potato mixture in prepared dish. Place dish in a shallow pan. Add hot water to pan to a depth of ¾" (about halfway up dish).

Bake at 325° for 1 hour or until a knife inserted in center comes out almost clean. Carefully remove dish from water. Cool custard on a wire rack. Cover and chill at least 8 hours.

Sprinkle custard with ⅓ cup brown sugar; place dish on a jellyroll pan. Broil 5½" from heat 3 to 5 minutes or until sugar melts. Let stand 5 minutes to allow sugar to harden before serving. Yield: 8 to 10 servings.

Tip: Removing a hot dish from a hot water bath can be tricky. We recommend wearing insulated rubber gloves to grasp the hot dish—they'll protect your hands from both the hot dish and hot water.

Sweet Potato Crème Brûlée

5-Star Choices
for Christmas Dinner

*Thoughts of turkey, dressing, and cranberry sauce flood our
minds as Christmas approaches. We offer festive updates to all
of your holiday favorites in this chapter. With new ideas for
entrées, sides, and desserts, we show you exciting ways to
impress family and friends all season long.*

THE MENU

Classic Roast Turkey and Gravy (page 111);
Cornbread Dressing Croquettes (page 119);
Cranberry-Orange Sauce (page 135);
Peas with Browned Butter, Caramelized
Onions, and Prosciutto (page 130); and
Sweet Potato Casserole (page 127)

. . . menu matters . . .

*We offer you a smorgasbord of options for every part of the menu so you can
mix and match the recipes to fit your family's preferences and your cooking style.
A classic holiday menu is shown at left. For more menu ideas, see page 183.*

Pick an entrée: *If turkey is your holiday mainstay,* we offer
three options: a classic roast turkey with rich brown gravy, a
turkey made extra moist and tender by an overnight soak in
an icy salt-water solution, and a blue-cheese stuffed breast
that serves a family of 6 to 8 nicely without lots of leftovers.
For temptations other than turkey, choose from among a mint-
filled, rolled, and roasted pork loin; a burgundy-baked ham;
a juicy tenderloin served with a cranberry-port reduction; or
simple but classic pecan-coated chicken breasts that cook in a
mere 20 minutes. Recipes start on page 111.

Pick a dressing: Dressing was never so festive. Choose
from our *classic cornbread* version with options for individual
croquettes or baking loaves to slice for the best leftover
turkey sandwiches you've ever tasted. *If convenience is key,*
try the recipes that dress up packaged stuffing mix. If you
want *something adventuresome,* try versions featuring
andouille sausage, oysters, sourdough bread, or wild rice.
Recipes start on page 119.

Pick a potato: *With ham or turkey and dressing on your
menu,* consider one of our four sweet potato recipes. Will it be
scalloped potatoes with a feisty chipotle sauce, plump sweet
potato hash brown patties, traditional mashed, or a fluffy
casserole? *With beef or pork loin on the plate,* opt for one of
our white potato recipes, such as traditional mashed or
mashed with accents of garlic-Gruyère or fennel, or Parmesan-
crusted rosemary potato wedges. Recipes begin on page 125.

Pick 1 to 4 vegetables: One veggie besides the potato
is really enough, but if you dare to add flair, consider three or
four. After all, it's Christmas! For color on the plate, *make
your selection a green one.* After that, *pick and choose from
your favorite vegetables* to round out the menu. Let oven
space, stovetop space, and oven temperatures play in your
decision. Recipes start on page 129.

Pick a cranberry: *The fruity flavor is a must for Christmas
dinner,* and it's expected as a chunky sauce alongside turkey

and dressing. Consider the relish or conserve if you serve
ham or pork loin. You'll enjoy cranberries with any entrée as
one of the salads, the muffin, or a light dessert ice recipe.
Our fave? Parmesan-crusted fried Brie appetizer balls with a
spicy dipping sauce. Recipes begin on page 135.

Ah, dessert! *Pick as many as you can fit into your schedule.*
Besides being the grand feast finale, leftovers are great for
late night family indulgences and to offer visitors. *Bold flavors*
like bittersweet chocolate, *great textures* like pecan pie with a
double thick crust, and *bright colors* as in cranberry meringue
pie offer options. Many of the recipes have *make-ahead* ideas
as well. Recipes begin on page 141.

THE ENTRÉE

Classic Roast Turkey and Gravy and
Cornbread Dressing Croquettes (page 119)

CLASSIC ROAST TURKEY AND GRAVY

For an evenly browned bird, turn the turkey's direction in the oven halfway through roasting, and baste often with pan drippings during the last 45 minutes. Make the gravy right in the roasting pan or transfer drippings to a saucepan.

1   (12-pound) turkey
1   bay leaf
2   celery ribs with leaves
1   small onion, quartered
Salt and pepper
½   cup butter, softened
1   teaspoon salt
½   teaspoon pepper
½   cup all-purpose flour
Salt and pepper to taste
Garnishes: bay leaves, Lady apples, Cornbread Dressing
     Croquettes (page 119)

Remove giblets and neck from turkey; place in a large saucepan, adding bay leaf, 1 celery rib, and half the onion. Add 6 cups water. Bring to a boil; reduce heat, and simmer, uncovered, 1 hour. Pour through a strainer. (You should yield 3 cups; add water if necessary to measure 3 cups.) Set aside.

Rinse turkey with cold water. Drain; pat dry. Sprinkle body cavity with salt and pepper; place remaining celery rib and onion inside cavity. Close cavity; tie ends of legs together with heavy string. Tuck wingtips under bird. Place turkey in a lightly greased roasting pan, breast side up. Rub turkey all over with 2 tablespoons softened butter; sprinkle with 1 teaspoon salt and ½ teaspoon pepper.

Roast, uncovered, at 325° until a meat thermometer reaches 180° in the thigh (about 3 hours), basting after 1 and 2 hours with remaining softened butter; turn turkey halfway through roasting. Baste frequently during last 45 minutes of cooking. Add 1 cup reserved turkey broth to roasting pan during last half hour of roasting. If turkey starts to brown too much, cover loosely with aluminum foil.

Let turkey rest in pan 5 minutes; carefully remove to a serving platter or carving board. Cover with foil, and let rest up to 45 minutes.

Meanwhile, prepare gravy. Skim excess fat from pan drippings, if desired. Working over medium heat on the stovetop, whisk flour into pan drippings until smooth. Whisking constantly, gradually add remaining 2 cups turkey broth; simmer 5 to 10 minutes or until gravy is thickened. Season with salt and pepper. Serve gravy with turkey. Garnish turkey, if desired. Yield: 8 to 10 servings.

Roasted Turkey with White Wine-Sage Sauce (at right), and Roasted Roots (page 133)

editor's favorite

ROASTED TURKEY WITH WHITE WINE-SAGE SAUCE

This turkey is butterflied so that it will roast quickly at a high temperature. It browns beautifully and still produces enough drippings for a delectable sauce. Brining is an extra step in this succulent recipe—well worth it when you taste the juicy results. Read about brining at left.

1   cup kosher salt
1   cup firmly packed light brown sugar
½   cup whole black peppercorns
1   (13-pound) fresh turkey
2   gallons water
1   (10-pound) bag crushed ice
2   tablespoons olive oil
1   tablespoon all-purpose flour
1½ cups pinot grigio wine
¼   cup fresh sage leaves, thinly sliced
¼   teaspoon freshly ground pepper
¼   cup whipping cream
Garnishes: fresh sage sprigs, Roasted Roots (page 133)

Combine first 3 ingredients in a bowl. Remove giblets and neck from turkey; reserve for other uses. Rinse turkey thoroughly with cold water. Drain body cavity well; pat dry. Rub 1 cup salt mixture over turkey and inside body and neck cavities.

Pour 1 gallon of water into a clean 28-quart cooler. Stir remaining salt mixture into water until dissolved. Place turkey, breast side down, in water. Add crushed ice. Pour remaining water over ice. Close cooler and soak turkey 12 hours.

Remove turkey from brine, discarding brine and unmelted ice. Rinse turkey for several minutes or until all traces of salt are gone; drain and pat dry with paper towels. Place turkey, breast side down, on a cutting board. Using heavy-duty kitchen shears, remove backbone, cutting down each side of bone. Open back of turkey; cut through breast bone with a sharp knife, splitting breast bone completely in half, but leaving breast skin and flesh intact. Turn turkey, breast side up, and press down firmly with heels of hands to flatten.

Place turkey, breast side up, on a rack in a large roasting pan. Tuck wings under, and press down on turkey breast to flatten as much as possible. Turn legs inward, placing knees against breasts. Brush or rub turkey with olive oil.

. . . brining a turkey . . .

Brining means to soak in a strong salt water solution. The benefits of brining are manyfold.

• The salty soak provides a tenderness cushion for the breast meat, so even if it overcooks by 10 degrees or so, it remains moist.

• The meat of a brined bird tastes pleasantly seasoned, which eliminates the need to season before and after roasting.

• Because the turkey sits overnight in a tub of salted water, brining also ensures that all parts of the turkey are at the same temperature. This is good insurance if you're roasting a previously frozen bird.

• The turkey meat absorbs water during the brining process. Water is a heat conductor and therefore expedites cooking. We tested this theory and found that indeed, a brined bird cooks faster than an unbrined one by about 30 minutes.

Roast, uncovered, at 450° for 1 hour and 40 minutes or until a meat thermometer inserted in thigh reaches 180°. Remove turkey to a carving board, reserving drippings in roasting pan. Cover turkey with aluminum foil; let rest 15 minutes.

Meanwhile, prepare sauce. Place roasting pan over 2 burners of stovetop. Whisk flour into drippings until smooth. Gradually whisk wine into drippings. Bring to a simmer over medium heat; cook, whisking constantly, 5 minutes or until sauce thickens. Stir in sage, pepper, and whipping cream; simmer 2 minutes or to desired consistency.

Carve legs and thighs from turkey, and place on a serving platter. Carve each turkey breast half from turkey in 1 whole piece. Cut breast halves crosswise into slices. Arrange breast slices on serving platter. Garnish, if desired. Serve turkey with sauce. Yield: 12 servings.

Note: Using a cooler to brine your bird frees up the refrigerator for all the other holiday foods.

BLUE CHEESE-STUFFED TURKEY BREAST

Blue cheese lovers will indulge in this heady version of a holiday favorite. The dark brown, rich sauce highlights beer, and is the perfect complement to the turkey roll.

6   ounces blue cheese, softened
¾   cup chopped dried apples
1¼ teaspoons freshly ground black pepper, divided
¾   teaspoon dried sage, divided
1   garlic clove, minced
1   (3-pound) boneless turkey breast
1   tablespoon butter, softened
½   teaspoon salt, divided
8   large shallots, peeled and quartered
1   teaspoon olive oil
1   (12-ounce) bottle Amber Draft Cider, divided
    (we tested with Woodchuck Amber Draft Cider)*
½   cup chicken broth
2   teaspoons cornstarch
2   tablespoons water

Combine blue cheese, apples, ¼ teaspoon pepper, ¼ teaspoon sage, and garlic in a small bowl. Set aside.

Remove and discard skin from turkey breast. Lay breast flat on heavy-duty plastic wrap (with what would have been skin side down). Starting from center, slice horizontally through thickest portion of each side of breast almost to, but not through, outer edges. Flip cut pieces over to enlarge breast. Place heavy-duty plastic wrap over turkey, and pound breast to flatten to ½" thickness, using a meat mallet or rolling pin.

Spread blue cheese mixture evenly over turkey breast to within 1" of edges; roll up turkey breast, jellyroll fashion, starting with short side. Tie securely at 1½" intervals with heavy string. Place turkey roll, seam side down, in a lightly greased shallow roasting pan.

Combine ½ teaspoon pepper, remaining ½ teaspoon sage, butter, and ¼ teaspoon salt in a small bowl. Rub evenly over turkey breast.

Toss shallots in olive oil. Arrange around turkey in pan.

Bake, uncovered, at 350° for 30 minutes. Baste turkey with ½ cup cider (pouring remaining amount from basting into pan). Bake 35 to 40 more minutes or until a thermometer registers 170°. Remove turkey, and cover with aluminum foil; let stand 10 minutes. Remove shallots, and set aside.

Add remaining cider to roasting pan, stirring to loosen any browned bits from bottom of pan. Pour mixture into a small saucepan. Add remaining ½ teaspoon pepper, remaining ¼ teaspoon salt, and chicken broth. Bring to a boil; reduce heat to medium, and simmer 5 minutes. Combine cornstarch and water; add to cider mixture. Return mixture to a boil, and cook, whisking constantly, 1 minute or until slightly thickened. Add shallots to sauce.

Remove string from turkey, and slice. Serve turkey with sauce. Yield: 6 to 8 servings.

* Single bottles of cider can often be purchased from a specialty beer and wine shop.

MINTED PORK LOIN

The aroma of mint, citrus, and onions in the spiral filling will lure you into the first bite of this rolled pork roast. It's a showy roast that will look lovely on a holiday table, ready to serve a large family.

3   medium-size sweet onions, chopped
3   garlic cloves, minced
1   tablespoon olive oil
½   cup tightly packed fresh mint, chopped
½   cup orange juice
2½ teaspoons salt, divided
2½ teaspoons freshly ground pepper, divided
1   (4-pound) boneless pork loin roast
1   tablespoon minced fresh rosemary
½   medium-size sweet onion, minced
1   tablespoon olive oil
Garnishes: fresh rosemary, fresh mint, orange slices

Sauté chopped onion and garlic in 1 tablespoon hot oil in a large skillet 8 minutes. Stir in mint, orange juice, ½ teaspoon salt, and ½ teaspoon pepper; cook, stirring often, 5 minutes or until orange juice evaporates.

Butterfly roast by making a lengthwise and horizontal cut down center of roast, cutting to within ½" of other side. Open roast, and place between 2 sheets of heavy-duty plastic wrap; flatten to ½" thickness, using a meat mallet or rolling pin.

Spread onion filling over roast, leaving a 1" margin around edges. Roll up roast; tie at 1" intervals with string.

Combine remaining 2 teaspoons salt, 2 teaspoons pepper, rosemary, minced onion, and 1 tablespoon oil. Spread over roast. Place on a rack in a roasting pan.

Bake, uncovered, at 450° for 15 minutes. Reduce to 350°; bake 1 hour and 15 minutes or until a meat thermometer inserted into thickest portion registers 160°.

Remove string. Let stand 10 minutes before slicing. Garnish, if desired. Yield: 8 to 10 servings.

Minted Pork Loin

Baked Burgundy Ham

BAKED BURGUNDY HAM

This sophisticated ham deserves to sit center stage on the holiday table. A tangy sweet marinade smothers it with flavor during baking. After baking, simmer the marinade to reduce it to a thick and glossy sauce to serve alongside.

1	(8-pound) smoked fully cooked ham half
6	cups water
2	cups cranberry-apple juice drink, divided
2	cups Burgundy or other dry red wine, divided
3	cups firmly packed dark brown sugar, divided
2	(3") cinnamon sticks
1	tablespoon whole cloves

Garnishes: Seckle pears, fresh bay leaves

Place ham in a large Dutch oven. Add water, 1 cup cranberry-apple juice drink, 1 cup wine, 1 cup brown sugar, cinnamon sticks, and cloves.

Bring to a boil; cover, reduce heat, and simmer 20 minutes. Remove from heat; cool. Remove ham and marinade from Dutch oven, and place in a large nonmetallic bowl. Cover and chill 8 hours, turning once after 4 hours.

Remove ham from marinade; reserve 2 cups marinade, and add 1 cup brown sugar. (Discard remaining marinade.) Place ham in a lightly greased shallow roasting pan.

Bake, uncovered, at 325° for 1½ hours, basting ham occasionally with reserved marinade mixture. Bake 20 minutes more or until meat thermometer registers 140°, basting ham occasionally with pan juices. Remove ham to a carving board, reserving pan juices.

Combine pan juices, remaining 1 cup cranberry-apple juice, 1 cup wine, and 1 cup brown sugar in a saucepan. Bring to a boil; reduce heat, and simmer, uncovered, until sauce thickens slightly and coats the back of a metal spoon (about 40 minutes). Serve sauce with ham. Garnish, if desired. Yield: 12 servings.

*Beef Tenderloin with Cranberry-Port
Reduction and Gorgonzola Butter*

BEEF TENDERLOIN WITH CRANBERRY-PORT REDUCTION AND GORGONZOLA BUTTER

Take a break from turkey and try this fancy beef entrée with two toppings.

1   (3½-pound) beef tenderloin
3   cups port or other sweet red wine
½   cup beef broth
4   shallots, peeled and halved
4   garlic cloves
2   teaspoons dried marjoram
½   cup whole-berry cranberry sauce
¼   teaspoon salt
¼   teaspoon pepper
Gorgonzola Butter
Garnishes: roasted baby carrots, roasted pearl onions

Secure tenderloin at 2" intervals with heavy string. Place tenderloin in a large zip-top freezer bag.

Combine port and next 4 ingredients; stir well. Pour marinade over tenderloin; seal. Marinate in refrigerator 2 hours, turning bag occasionally.

Remove tenderloin from marinade, reserving marinade. Pour liquid through a wire-mesh strainer into a bowl; reserve garlic and discard solids. Set 1 cup marinade aside.

Place tenderloin on a lightly greased broiler pan. Insert a meat thermometer into thickest portion of tenderloin. Place tenderloin in a preheated 425° oven. Immediately reduce heat to 350°; bake, uncovered, for 1 hour or until thermometer registers 145° (medium rare) to 160° (medium) or to desired degree of doneness. Let stand 10 minutes before slicing. Remove string.

Combine reserved garlic and 1 cup reserved marinade in a small saucepan; bring to a boil. Reduce heat, and simmer 8 minutes or until reduced by half. Remove and discard garlic. Stir in cranberry sauce, salt, and pepper. Bring to a boil; cover and simmer 1 minute. Garnish, if desired. Serve with Cranberry-Port Reduction and Gorgonzola Butter. Yield: 12 servings.

GORGONZOLA BUTTER

Save time and enhance the flavor of this creamy butter by making it a day ahead and chilling it overnight.

4   ounces Gorgonzola or blue cheese
¼   cup butter or margarine, softened
1   tablespoon minced fresh chives

Beat cheese and butter at medium speed with an electric mixer until blended. Stir in chives. Spoon into a crock, or if desired, spoon butter mixture onto plastic wrap. Shape butter into a 1" diameter log by folding wrap over mixture and rolling. (Work quickly to keep butter from melting.) Seal plastic wrap, and chill 4 hours or until firm. Yield: about ¾ cup.

Note: To roast the vegetables for garnish, drizzle lightly with olive oil, and sprinkle with salt and pepper. Roast at 450° for 15 minutes, stirring once.

editor's favorite

PECAN CHICKEN WITH HONEY-MUSTARD SAUCE

Serve this dressed-up chicken dish with a wild rice blend and a crisp green salad.

3   tablespoons stone-ground mustard
4   skinned and boned chicken breasts
1   cup pecan pieces, coarsely ground
¼   teaspoon ground red pepper
1½   tablespoons butter
1½   tablespoons vegetable oil
1½   cups whipping cream
2   tablespoons honey
2   tablespoons stone-ground mustard
¼   teaspoon salt

Spread 3 tablespoons mustard on each side of chicken. Combine ground pecans and red pepper in a shallow bowl. Gently coat chicken with pecan mixture.

Heat butter and oil in a large skillet until hot. Add chicken; cook over medium-high heat 2 minutes on each side or just until browned. Place in a greased 11" x 7" baking dish. Bake, uncovered, at 375° for 15 minutes or until done.

Heat whipping cream in large skillet over medium-high heat until reduced by half (about 12 minutes). Stir in honey, 2 tablespoons mustard, and salt. Serve sauce with chicken. Yield: 4 servings.

THE DRESSING

Fruited Wild Rice Dressing (page 122)

This dressing recipe looks a little soupy when you mix it, but the end result is wonderfully moist. If you like yours a little drier, cut down on the chicken broth. And if you are "antisage" (some folks prefer poultry seasoning), you can reduce it, omit it, or substitute 1 teaspoon poultry seasoning. However, if you've based your judgment on the dried variety, try fresh sage before omitting it. It gives the dressing a more delicate flavor.

editor's favorite

CORNBREAD DRESSING

1   cup butter or margarine, divided
3   cups white cornmeal
1   cup all-purpose flour
2   tablespoons sugar
2   teaspoons baking powder
1½ teaspoons salt
1   teaspoon baking soda
7   large eggs
3   cups buttermilk
3   cups soft breadcrumbs (we tested with 6 slices Pepperidge Farm white sandwich bread)
2   medium onions, diced (2 cups)
1   large bunch celery, diced (3 cups)
½   cup finely chopped fresh sage
6   (10½-ounce) cans condensed chicken broth, undiluted
1   tablespoon pepper

Place ½ cup butter in a 13" x 9" pan; heat in oven at 425° for 4 minutes.

Combine cornmeal and next 5 ingredients; whisk in 3 eggs and buttermilk.

Pour hot butter into batter, stirring until blended. Pour batter into pan.

Bake, uncovered, at 425° for 30 minutes or until golden brown. Cool. Crumble cornbread into a large bowl; stir in breadcrumbs, and set aside.

Melt remaining ½ cup butter in a skillet over medium heat; add onion and celery, and sauté until tender. Stir in sage; sauté 1 minute. Stir vegetables, remaining 4 eggs, chicken broth, and pepper into cornbread mixture; pour into 1 lightly greased 13" x 9" baking dish and 1 lightly greased 8" square baking dish. Cover and chill 8 hours.

Bake, uncovered, at 375° for 1 hour and 5 minutes or until golden brown. Yield: 16 to 18 servings.

. . . dressing variations . . .

Cornbread Dressing Croquettes: (photo on pages 110-111) Use only 2 cans of chicken broth for this recipe. Shape unbaked dressing into croquettes, using a ¼ cup ice cream scoop. Place croquettes on lightly greased baking sheets, making sure not to crowd them on the sheets. Bake at 400° for 30 minutes or until well browned (and internal temperature reaches 160°). Cool on baking sheets 10 minutes. Yield: 4 dozen.

Cornbread Dressing Loaf: Use only 2 cans of chicken broth for this recipe. Fill a lightly greased 9" x 5" loafpan with 8 cups unbaked cornbread dressing. (Prepare Cornbread Dressing Croquettes with remaining dressing.) Press into pan firmly; invert dressing loaf onto a baking sheet, and remove pan. Bake at 375° for 1½ hours (or until internal temperature reaches 160°). Cool overnight. Slice into ½" slices. Place on lightly greased baking sheet. Bake at 425° for 30 minutes. Cool completely on baking sheet. Top toasted cornbread slices with turkey and cranberry sauce and your favorite sandwich fixin's.

DRESSING CROUTONS

Serve these herby croutons with cranberry sauce or Ranch dressing as an appetizer or snack.

¼	cup butter
2	celery ribs, chopped
½	large onion, chopped
3	green onions, chopped
5	cups crumbled cornbread
2	large eggs, lightly beaten
1	(8-ounce) package herb-seasoned stuffing mix
3	cups chicken broth

Melt butter in a large skillet over medium-high heat. Add celery and onions; cook 5 minutes or until tender. Remove from heat. Combine onion mixture, cornbread, and next 3 ingredients in a large bowl; mix well. Spread cornbread mixture into a lightly greased jellyroll pan.

Bake at 350° for 30 to 33 minutes or until set. Cool on a wire rack 30 minutes. Refrigerate 1 to 2 hours or until chilled.

Loosen edges of cornbread dressing with a sharp knife. Turn out onto a large cutting board. Cut into ¾" cubes. Place in a single layer on greased large baking sheets. Bake at 450° for 35 to 40 minutes, turning occasionally, or until well browned and crisp. Yield: 10 cups.

Dressing Croutons

Herb and Garlic Dressing Soufflé

HERB AND GARLIC DRESSING SOUFFLÉ

To "heighten" the effect of this soufflé, use a 1½-quart soufflé dish, allowing the soufflé to puff for presentation.

3   tablespoons butter, divided
2½ cups soft breadcrumbs, divided
3   large garlic cloves, minced
2   large shallots, minced
¼   cup chopped fresh parsley
¼   cup chopped fresh chives
1   tablespoon chopped fresh sage
1   tablespoon chopped fresh thyme
2   teaspoons chopped fresh rosemary
¾   teaspoon salt
¼   teaspoon ground white pepper
1   (8-ounce) package cream cheese,
    softened
6   large eggs, separated
1   cup milk

Brush a 1½- or 2-quart soufflé dish with 2 tablespoons butter; dust with ½ cup breadcrumbs.

Melt remaining 1 tablespoon butter in a small skillet over medium-high heat. Add garlic and shallots; cook 2 minutes or until tender. Stir in parsley and next 6 ingredients.

Beat cream cheese at medium speed with an electric mixer until creamy. Add yolks, beating well. Add garlic mixture; beat well.

Heat milk in a large heavy saucepan over medium heat until tiny bubbles begin to appear around edges of pan. Gradually whisk about one-fourth of hot milk into yolk mixture; add to remaining hot milk. Cook over medium heat 4 minutes or until thickened and thermometer registers 160°, whisking constantly.

Transfer yolk mixture to a large bowl; gently fold in remaining 2 cups breadcrumbs.

Beat egg whites at high speed with an electric mixer until soft peaks form; gently fold into yolk mixture.

Pour egg mixture into prepared dish. Bake at 350° for 30 to 35 minutes or until puffed and golden. Serve immediately. Yield: 8 servings.

APPLE-CABBAGE DRESSING

1½ (16-ounce) loaves sliced rye bread (we tested with
     Pepperidge Farm)
¾   pound coarsely chopped cabbage (about ½ small)
2   medium cooking apples, diced (about 2¼ cups)
1   cup chopped onion
3   celery ribs, diced
4   garlic cloves, minced
½   cup butter or margarine, melted and divided
1   teaspoon salt
½   teaspoon pepper
1   cup apple cider or apple juice
1   cup chicken broth

Place bread slices in single layers on 2 baking sheets. Bake at 325° for 25 minutes or until almost crisp, using both racks in oven. Tear bread into small pieces, and place in a 4-quart bowl.

Bring 8 cups water to a boil in a Dutch oven; add cabbage, and cook, uncovered, 3 minutes. Drain and immediately run cold water over cabbage; pat dry with paper towels. Add to bread in bowl, and set aside.

Cook apple, onion, celery, and garlic in ¼ cup butter in a large skillet over medium heat 10 minutes or until tender, stirring often. Add apple mixture to cabbage; stir in salt and pepper.

Pour cider and broth over bread mixture, tossing gently. Spoon mixture into a buttered 13" x 9" baking dish; drizzle with remaining ¼ cup melted butter. Bake, uncovered, at 350° for 40 minutes or until lightly browned. Yield: 12 servings.

SOURDOUGH-OYSTER DRESSING

8   cups cubed sourdough bread (about 8 slices)
¼   cup butter or margarine
1   onion, finely chopped
4   celery ribs, chopped
2   garlic cloves, minced
1   teaspoon salt
½   teaspoon ground black pepper
1   (8-ounce) container shucked oysters, drained and
     coarsely chopped (about 2 dozen oysters)
½   cup whipping cream
8   bacon slices, cooked and crumbled
⅓   cup chopped fresh Italian parsley
1   (6-ounce) jar marinated artichoke hearts, drained
     and chopped

Arrange bread cubes on 2 baking sheets. Bake at 350°
for 10 minutes or until dry and golden.

Melt butter in a large skillet over medium-high heat;
add onion, celery, and garlic. Sauté 6 to 8 minutes or
until tender. Add salt and next 3 ingredients; cook 1
minute. Remove from heat.

Combine bread cubes, oyster mixture, bacon, parsley,
and artichoke hearts in a large bowl, tossing well. Spoon
dressing into a greased 11" x 7" baking dish. Bake,
uncovered, at 375° for 45 minutes. Yield: 8 servings.

FRUITED WILD RICE DRESSING

*Dried fruits add sweetness and color to this dressing that's
equally at home with turkey, chicken, or pork.*

1   (6-ounce) package long-grain and wild
     rice mix
6   cups (½" cubes) country-style bread (we tested
     with Italian ciabatta)
1   pound ground pork sausage
2   small onions, chopped
4   celery ribs, chopped
¼   cup butter
1   cup dried apricots, coarsely chopped
¾   cup dried cherries
½   cup chopped fresh Italian parsley
½   teaspoon salt
½   teaspoon pepper
1   cup chicken broth

*Fruited Wild
Rice Dressing*

Prepare rice mix according to package directions.
Transfer to a large bowl, and fluff with a fork. Set aside.

Place bread cubes on a large-rimmed pan and toast at
325° for 20 minutes or until dry. Set aside.

Cook sausage in a large skillet over medium heat,
stirring until it crumbles and is well browned; drain.

Sauté onion and celery in butter in a large skillet over
medium heat until tender.

Combine rice, bread, sausage, sautéed vegetables,
dried fruit, parsley, salt, and pepper in a large bowl;
toss well. Drizzle broth evenly over dressing. Toss
well. Transfer dressing to a lightly greased 3-quart
baking dish.

Bake, covered, at 375° for 20 minutes. Uncover and
bake 25 to 30 more minutes or until browned. Yield: 8 to
10 servings.

editor's favorite

GREEN CHILE-CHEDDAR-PECAN DRESSING

This dressing sports favorite Southern flavors from pecans and cornbread, and gets a kick from green chiles.

1   cup pecan pieces
2   tablespoons butter, melted
½   teaspoon garlic powder
¼   teaspoon salt
1   teaspoon paprika
¼   teaspoon ground red pepper
1   (8-ounce) package shredded sharp Cheddar cheese, divided
7   cups cornbread crumbs*
6   cups biscuit crumbs (we tested with Pillsbury Frozen Buttermilk Biscuits)
1   (15.25-ounce) can sweet whole kernel corn, drained
1   (4.5-ounce) can chopped green chiles, drained
2   large eggs, lightly beaten
¼   cup chopped fresh cilantro
½   teaspoon salt
½   teaspoon dried oregano
¼   teaspoon black pepper
3½   cups chicken broth
Garnish: fresh cilantro

Combine first 6 ingredients in a small bowl, tossing well. Spread in a single layer on a baking sheet. Bake at 350° for 10 minutes or until toasted; set aside.

Combine 1½ cups cheese and next 9 ingredients in a large bowl. Add broth, stirring just until moistened. Spoon dressing into a lightly greased 13" x 9" baking dish. Sprinkle with remaining ½ cup cheese and reserved pecans.

Bake, uncovered, at 350° for 50 to 55 minutes or until set and lightly browned. Garnish, if desired. Yield: 12 servings.

* 1 (28-ounce) package of frozen Sister Schubert's Southern Cornbread is equivalent to the 7 cups of cornbread crumbs needed in this recipe. Otherwise, look for baked cornbread in your supermarket deli.

editor's favorite

ANDOUILLE DRESSING

An andouille-laced dressing highlights the Cajun trinity of celery, onion, and green pepper.

½   cup butter
1   (1-pound) package Cajun-style cooked andouille sausage, diced
3   cups diced onion
2   cups diced celery
2   cups diced green bell pepper
2   garlic cloves, minced
2   teaspoons rubbed sage
1   teaspoon dried thyme
½   teaspoon salt
½   teaspoon pepper
1   (16-ounce) package cornbread stuffing mix
4   cups chicken broth

Melt butter in a large nonstick skillet over medium-high heat. Add sausage; cook 4 minutes or until browned. Transfer sausage to a large bowl, reserving drippings in skillet.

Add onion and next 7 ingredients to skillet; cook 8 minutes or until tender, stirring occasionally. Add vegetables and stuffing mix to sausage. Add broth, stirring just until moistened.

Spoon dressing into a greased 15" x 10" roasting pan.

Bake, covered, at 350° for 30 minutes. Uncover and bake 20 more minutes. Yield: 12 servings.

Green Chile-Cheddar-Pecan Dressing

THE POTATOES

Garlic-Gruyère Mashed
Potatoes, Cider Mashed Sweet
Potatoes, and Mashed Potatoes
with Fennel (all on page 126)

PARMESAN-ROSEMARY POTATOES

The cheese and herb coating makes these potatoes addictive.
Use the coating for chicken breasts or pork chops, too.

3   pounds baking potatoes
3   cups cold water
1   teaspoon salt
1   cup butter, melted
Parmesan-Rosemary Coating
Salt
Garnish: fresh rosemary

Wash potatoes. Cut potatoes in half lengthwise; slice potato halves crosswise into half moon-shaped wedges.

Combine water and 1 teaspoon salt in a large bowl; add potatoes, and let stand 5 minutes. Drain well; spread potatoes on paper towels to absorb water. Pat dry.

Dip potato wedges in butter; roll in Parmesan-Rosemary Coating. Place in a single layer on a lightly greased baking sheet. Bake at 400° for 40 minutes or until potatoes are tender and golden brown. Sprinkle lightly with salt before serving. Garnish, if desired. Yield: 6 to 8 servings.

PARMESAN-ROSEMARY COATING

1   cup finely shredded Parmesan cheese
½   cup fine, dry breadcrumbs
2½   tablespoons finely chopped fresh rosemary
1   teaspoon salt
½   teaspoon garlic powder
¼   teaspoon pepper

Combine all ingredients in a medium bowl. Yield: 1⅔ cups.

Parmesan-Rosemary Potatoes

. . . solid gold . . .

If you're unfamiliar with Yukon gold potatoes, there's a reason. Yukon golds are relatively new to North America; they were first introduced in 1980 . . . lucky for us!

Yukon gold potatoes are a yellow-fleshed potato, known for their buttery flavor and creamy texture. Quite versatile, they can be used for baking, broiling, or frying—but we particularly like them mashed.

HOMESTYLE MASHED POTATOES

One of the keys to fluffy spuds is returning the cooked potatoes to the warm, dry pan you cooked them in for mashing.

2   pounds medium potatoes, peeled and quartered
      (we tested with Yukon gold)
¼   cup butter or margarine
½   cup whipping cream
1   teaspoon salt
½   teaspoon freshly ground pepper

Cook potato in boiling water to cover 20 to 25 minutes or until very tender. Drain well, and return potato to pan. Add butter, and mash until butter melts, using a potato masher. Add cream, salt, and pepper; mash to desired texture. Yield: 6 servings.

GARLIC-GRUYÈRE MASHED POTATOES

(photo on page 124)

Gruyère cheese makes these mashed potatoes rich. Sour cream, garlic, and green onions give them unforgettable status.

3   pounds Yukon gold potatoes (about 7 large)
¼   cup butter or margarine, softened
¾   cup hot milk
½   cup sour cream
¾   teaspoon salt
¼   teaspoon pepper
1   garlic clove, minced
1   cup (4 ounces) shredded Gruyère cheese or other Swiss cheese
2   green onions, thinly sliced
Garnishes: additional diagonally sliced green onions, shredded Gruyère cheese

Peel potatoes, if desired; cut into chunks. Cook in boiling water to cover 15 to 20 minutes or until tender. Drain well. Return potatoes to pan. Add butter.

Mash with a potato masher; stir in hot milk and next 4 ingredients. Mash again to desired texture.

Stir in 1 cup cheese and 2 thinly sliced green onions. Garnish, if desired. Yield: 8 servings.

MASHED POTATOES WITH FENNEL

(photo on page 124)

Cooked fennel takes on a slightly sweet note that adds a sublime flavor to these creamy potatoes.

3   pounds fennel
1½   cups half-and-half
1½   pounds Yukon gold potatoes, peeled and cubed (about 4 medium)
¼   cup butter, softened
1   teaspoon salt
½   teaspoon freshly ground black pepper

Trim bases from fennel bulbs; reserve fronds for garnish. Cut each bulb in half through base. Cut out core from each half. Slice fennel lengthwise into ¼" slices; cut slices in half crosswise.

Combine fennel and half-and-half in a medium saucepan. Bring to a boil; reduce heat, and simmer 25 to 30 minutes or until fennel is very soft. Drain fennel, reserving cooking liquid. Place fennel and 2 tablespoons cooking liquid in a blender or food processor; process 30 to 45 seconds or until smooth.

Meanwhile, bring potato and water to cover to a boil in a large saucepan; cook 15 to 20 minutes or until tender. Drain potatoes, and return to saucepan. Add butter, fennel puree, salt, and pepper; mash well with a potato masher or hand mixer until smooth. For creamier potatoes, add reserved cooking liquid, 1 tablespoon at a time, to desired texture. Garnish with chopped fennel fronds, if desired. Yield: 4 cups.

CIDER MASHED SWEET POTATOES

(photo on page 124)

Apple cider enhances this simple sweet potato side dish.

2   pounds sweet potatoes (about 3 large)
1   cup apple cider
1   large Braeburn apple, peeled and coarsely chopped
¼   cup butter, softened
1   tablespoon light brown sugar
¾   teaspoon salt
¼   teaspoon ground cinnamon
Dash of nutmeg

Pierce potatoes several times with a fork. Bake at 375° for 1 hour or until very soft; cool slightly.

Meanwhile, bring apple cider and chopped apple to a boil in a small saucepan; reduce heat, and simmer 12 to 15 minutes or until apple is very soft (apple may begin to lose its shape). Drain apple, reserving cooking liquid. Return liquid to saucepan; simmer over medium heat for 6 to 8 more minutes or until thickened to the consistency of syrup.

Cut potatoes in half lengthwise; scoop out pulp, and place in a large bowl. Discard shells. Add cooked apple to potatoes; mash with a potato masher until blended. Add butter and next 4 ingredients; continue mashing, adding reserved cooking liquid, until potatoes are desired texture. Serve hot. Yield: 4 to 6 servings.

SWEET POTATO GRATIN WITH CHIPOTLE SAUCE

Smoky chipotle peppers make this scalloped potato casserole memorable.

3½ pounds sweet potatoes
¼ cup butter
¾ cup chopped onion
2 garlic cloves, minced
¼ cup all-purpose flour
2½ cups half-and-half
1½ teaspoons salt
½ teaspoon ground cumin
¼ teaspoon pepper
3 cups (12 ounces) shredded Monterey Jack cheese
1½ tablespoons finely chopped chipotle peppers in adobo sauce (about 3 chiles)

Cook sweet potatoes in boiling water to cover 20 minutes or until barely tender. Drain and let cool slightly. Peel potatoes, and cut crosswise into ½" slices. Layer potatoes in a lightly greased 13" x 9" baking dish or oval gratin dish.

Melt butter in a saucepan over medium heat; add onion and garlic, and sauté until tender. Sprinkle flour over onion mixture; cook 1 minute, stirring constantly. Gradually add half-and-half, stirring constantly until thickened and bubbly. Stir in salt, cumin, and pepper. Add cheese and chipotle peppers, stirring until cheese melts.

Pour cheese sauce over potatoes. Bake, uncovered, at 350° for 45 minutes or until lightly browned and bubbly. Let stand 15 minutes before serving. Yield: 12 servings.

editor's favorite
SWEET POTATO CASSEROLE

Blending this sweet potato filling in a food processor is the key to creamy results. This simple, classic Southern side dish earned our highest rating.

3½ cups cooked mashed sweet potatoes*
½ cup butter, melted
¼ cup milk
2 large eggs
1 cup sugar
1 teaspoon vanilla extract
3½ cups miniature marshmallows

Process first 3 ingredients in a food processor until very smooth, about 2 minutes. Add eggs, sugar, and vanilla; process until blended. Pour into a greased 13" x 9" baking dish.

Cover and bake at 350° for 15 minutes; uncover and sprinkle with marshmallows. Bake, uncovered, 20 more minutes or until marshmallows are toasted. Serve hot. Yield: 8 servings.

* For best results, we recommend buying and cooking 3 large, deep orange sweet potatoes. Cut them in half crosswise; boil them in their skins 35 to 37 minutes or until very tender. Cool and slip potatoes out of their skins. Mash with a potato masher to equal 3½ cups. In a pinch, use 2 (29-ounce) cans candied yams as a substitute. Each (29-ounce) can yields 2 cups mashed.

SWEET POTATO HASH BROWNS

To save a little time, substitute precooked bacon for the bacon slices, if desired.

1 teaspoon butter or margarine
2 tablespoons vegetable oil, divided
1 medium onion, diced
1 tablespoon light brown sugar
1 medium-size baking potato, peeled and shredded
1 medium-size sweet potato, peeled and shredded
1 large egg, lightly beaten
3 tablespoons all-purpose flour
½ teaspoon salt
½ teaspoon pepper
4 bacon slices, cooked and crumbled

Melt butter and 1 tablespoon oil in a large nonstick skillet over medium heat. Add onion; sauté 15 minutes or until golden. Add brown sugar, and cook 5 minutes, stirring often.

Stir together onion, potatoes, and next 5 ingredients in a large bowl.

Heat remaining 1 tablespoon oil in a large nonstick skillet over medium-high heat. Drop ¼ cupfuls potato mixture into skillet for each pancake. Cook pancakes, in batches, 5 minutes on each side or until golden, pressing down with a spatula to flatten. Serve warm. Yield: 8 pancakes.

THE VEGETABLES

Roasted Broccoli with Buttered Walnuts

quick & easy

ROASTED BROCCOLI WITH BUTTERED WALNUTS

3   pounds fresh broccoli
⅓   cup olive oil
1   teaspoon salt
½   teaspoon pepper
1   cup walnut halves
3   tablespoons butter, melted
1   lemon, halved

Cut broccoli into 3" lengths; cut thick pieces in half lengthwise. Place in a roasting pan, and drizzle with olive oil; toss to coat well. Sprinkle with salt and pepper. Roast at 500° for 14 minutes, stirring once after 8 minutes.

Meanwhile, toast walnuts in melted butter in a skillet over medium-high heat 5 minutes or until fragrant.

Spoon broccoli into a serving bowl. Squeeze cut lemon over broccoli, tossing well. Stir in walnuts and butter. Yield: 6 to 8 servings.

BRUSSELS SPROUTS AND WILD RICE

Quick-cooking wild rice is a real time-saver. You'll need about 3 cups cooked rice for this recipe.

2½   cups water
1   (½-ounce) package dried morel mushrooms
2   (16-ounce) packages fresh Brussels sprouts
2   cups chicken broth
1   (6-ounce) package uncooked wild rice
¼   cup butter, divided
½   cup chopped leeks
3   tablespoons water
1   teaspoon salt
¼   teaspoon pepper

Combine water and mushrooms in a large saucepan; bring to a boil. Cover, reduce heat, and simmer 2 minutes. Remove from heat; let stand 30 minutes. Drain mushrooms, reserving 1 cup liquid. Coarsely chop mushrooms.

Wash Brussels sprouts thoroughly, and remove discolored leaves. Trim stem ends, and cut in half; set aside.

Combine chicken broth and 1 cup reserved liquid in same saucepan; bring to a boil. Add rice and mushrooms. Cover and simmer 50 minutes. Remove from heat; drain.

Melt 2 tablespoons butter in a large nonstick skillet over medium-high heat; add leeks. Sauté 3 minutes or until tender. Remove from skillet; set aside. Melt remaining butter in skillet over medium-high heat; add Brussels sprouts, and sauté 5 minutes or until browned. Add 3 tablespoons water; cover and cook 5 to 6 minutes or until Brussels sprouts are fork-tender, adding more water as necessary.

Add cooked rice, leeks, salt, and pepper; stir gently. Cook over medium-low heat just until thoroughly heated. Yield: 8 to 10 servings.

HONEY-GLAZED CRANBERRY CARROTS

A simple carrot dish like this is a bonus for the busy holiday cook.

½   cup fresh orange juice
⅓   cup dried cranberries
¼   cup butter
2   tablespoons honey
1   tablespoon grated fresh ginger
2   pounds carrots

Combine first 5 ingredients in a small saucepan. Bring to a boil over medium-high heat, stirring constantly. Boil 15 to 20 minutes or until glaze is thickened and coats the back of a spoon.

Meanwhile, peel carrots, and slice into ¼" diagonal slices. Place carrot in a large saucepan with water to cover. Bring to a boil. Cover and cook 12 minutes or until tender. Drain well. Add carrot to honey-cranberry mixture; toss well. Yield: 4 cups.

Honey-Glazed Cranberry Carrots

Peas with Browned Butter, Caramelized Onions, and Prosciutto

PEAS WITH BROWNED BUTTER, CARAMELIZED ONIONS, AND PROSCIUTTO

Peas get dressed up here with browned butter and Italian ham.

1   (16-ounce) package frozen sweet peas
½   cup chicken broth
3   ounces thinly sliced prosciutto
¼   cup butter, divided
1   tablespoon olive oil
1½ cups chopped onion
1   tablespoon sugar
1   tablespoon balsamic vinegar
¼   teaspoon dried thyme
¼   teaspoon pepper

Cook peas according to package directions, substituting ½ cup broth for water. Drain; set aside in a serving bowl, and keep warm.

Cook prosciutto in a large skillet over medium-high heat until crisp. Remove prosciutto from pan; cool and coarsely crumble.

Melt 1 tablespoon butter with oil in large skillet over medium-high heat. Add onion; cook 28 minutes or until golden, stirring occasionally.

While onions cook, melt remaining 3 tablespoons butter in a small saucepan over medium-low heat. Cook 5 minutes or until butter is browned, stirring occasionally. Stir sugar, vinegar, thyme, and pepper into onion; cook 2 more minutes. Remove from heat. Stir caramelized onion and crumbled prosciutto into peas. Pour browned butter over peas. Serve warm. Yield: 4 servings.

CREAMED ONION GRATIN

These are some of the best creamed onions ever to pass through our Test Kitchens. With a crusty top and white Cheddar sauce—what's not to love?

2   (10-ounce) packages fresh pearl onions, peeled
2   tablespoons butter
2   tablespoons all-purpose flour
1¼ cups half-and-half
½   teaspoon salt
½   teaspoon freshly ground black pepper
¼   teaspoon ground mustard
Dash of ground nutmeg
1½ cups (6 ounces) shredded white Cheddar cheese, divided
1¼ cups fresh breadcrumbs*
2   tablespoons butter, melted
1   teaspoon chopped fresh thyme

Place onions in a large saucepan; add water to cover. Bring to boil; reduce heat, and simmer 6 to 8 minutes or until onions are just tender. Drain well. Set aside.

Melt 2 tablespoons butter in a heavy saucepan over low heat; add flour, stirring until smooth. Cook 1 minute, stirring constantly. Gradually add half-and-half; cook over medium heat, stirring constantly, until thickened. Add salt and next 3 ingredients. Add 1 cup shredded cheese; stir until cheese melts. Gently stir in drained onions. Pour onion mixture into a lightly greased 1-quart baking dish. Sprinkle evenly with remaining ½ cup shredded cheese.

Toss breadcrumbs with melted butter and thyme until crumbs are well coated. Sprinkle evenly over cheese.

Bake, uncovered, at 350° for 25 to 30 minutes or until thoroughly heated and top is golden. Yield: 6 to 8 servings.

* Pulse 3 bread slices in a mini food chopper or food processor. It should yield 1¼ cups breadcrumbs.

Creamed Onion Gratin

Roasted Roots

Roasted Roots

If your parsnips are wide at the root end, cut chunks in half lengthwise for even cooking. Be careful not to crowd veggies in the pan—it will hinder their browning. Use two pans, if necessary, to prevent crowding.

1½ pounds carrots, peeled and cut into 1½" chunks
1½ pounds parsnips, peeled and cut into 1½" chunks
3   tablespoons olive oil
1   tablespoon sugar
1½ teaspoons kosher salt
½   teaspoon freshly ground pepper

Combine all ingredients in a shallow roasting pan or broiler pan; toss well, and spread in a single layer. Roast at 475° for 30 minutes, stirring after 25 minutes. Yield: 4 to 6 servings.

editor's favorite • quick & easy

Fontina Grits and Collards

This recipe reflects a New South twist on collards.

¾   pound collard greens
¼   cup butter or margarine
1   cup finely chopped sweet onion
2   tablespoons water
1½ cups chicken broth
1¼ cups heavy whipping cream
½   cup uncooked quick-cooking grits
½   pound fontina cheese, cut into small cubes

Wash collard greens thoroughly, and cut off stems. Stack leaves; roll up lengthwise. Cut 2 lengthwise slits down leaves; cut crosswise into ¼" strips, and set aside.

Melt butter over medium heat in a saucepan. Add onion; sauté 3 minutes or until tender. Add collard greens; sprinkle with water, and cook, covered, 4 to 5 minutes or until greens are tender.

Combine broth and cream in a large saucepan; bring to a simmer over medium heat. Reduce heat to low; stir in grits, and cook, uncovered, 10 minutes. Add cheese; stir until melted. Stir in cooked collard greens. Yield: 4 to 6 servings.

Four-Cheese Spinach Macaroni

You may never crave traditional mac-and-cheese again after tasting this creamy, cheesy garlic-and-spinach version with penne pasta.

12 ounces penne pasta
2   tablespoons butter or margarine
2   garlic cloves, pressed
2   cups milk
1   cup (4 ounces) shredded Parmesan cheese, divided
1   (8-ounce) package cream cheese, softened
1   (8-ounce) container mascarpone cheese
1   (4-ounce) package crumbled Gorgonzola cheese
1   teaspoon salt
1   teaspoon ground white pepper
¼   teaspoon ground nutmeg
1   (10-ounce) package frozen chopped spinach, thawed and well drained
1   cup soft breadcrumbs
2   tablespoons butter or margarine, melted

Cook pasta according to package directions, and drain. Meanwhile, melt 2 tablespoons butter in a Dutch oven over medium heat; add garlic, and sauté 1 minute. Add milk, and cook until thoroughly heated. Gradually stir in ½ cup Parmesan cheese and next 6 ingredients; whisk until smooth. Stir in spinach. Add cooked pasta, tossing to coat. Spoon into a lightly greased 13" x 9" baking dish.

Combine breadcrumbs, remaining ½ cup Parmesan cheese, and 2 tablespoons melted butter in a small bowl. Sprinkle breadcrumb topping over macaroni. Bake, uncovered, at 375° for 20 minutes or until golden. Yield: 8 servings.

Fresh Spinach Substitution: You can substitute a 10-ounce package of fresh spinach instead of using frozen spinach, if desired. Just wash the spinach, trim stems, and coarsely chop the leaves. Then wilt the leaves for 1 to 2 minutes in hot water in a pan.

THE CRANBERRIES

Brie Balls with Spicy
Cranberry Dipping Sauce

We call for fresh cranberries, dried cranberries, and sweetened dried cranberries in these recipes. For the sweetened version, we tested with Craisins. Each one serves a distinct flavor purpose in each dish.

make ahead
CRANBERRY-ORANGE SAUCE

This cranberry sauce recipe makes a lot, so you'll have plenty to serve alongside turkey, on sandwiches, or as a sauce drizzled over cheesecake or ice cream.

2   (12-ounce) packages fresh cranberries
2   cups granulated sugar
½   cup firmly packed light brown sugar
2   teaspoons grated orange rind
⅓   cup fresh orange juice
2   (3") cinnamon sticks
½   teaspoon ground ginger
2   large navel oranges, peeled, sectioned, and chopped
¼   cup port wine

Stir together first 8 ingredients in a large saucepan; bring to a boil over medium-high heat, stirring often. Reduce heat; simmer 15 minutes or until cranberries pop and mixture starts to thicken, stirring often. Remove from heat. Discard cinnamon sticks. Stir in wine. Cool. Cover and chill until ready to serve. Yield: 6¼ cups.

make ahead
ICED CRANBERRY SAUCE

For a refreshing twist on the classic cranberry condiment, try this slushy cranberry sauce. Serve it in little stemmed cordials or other tiny glasses.

2   cups water
1   (12-ounce) package fresh cranberries
1½ cups sugar
2   tablespoons fresh lemon juice
1   teaspoon grated orange rind
½   cup fresh orange juice
1   teaspoon finely chopped fresh rosemary

Combine water and cranberries in a large saucepan. Bring to a boil over high heat; boil 8 to 10 minutes or until skins pop. Remove from heat. Process cranberries, in batches, in a food processor until coarsely pureed. Press pureed cranberries through a wire-mesh strainer into a bowl, discarding solids. Add sugar and remaining 4 ingredients to cranberry puree, stirring until sugar dissolves.

Divide cranberry sauce evenly among 6 (6-ounce) custard cups or ramekins. Cover and freeze until firm. Remove from freezer 10 to 15 minutes before serving. Yield: 6 servings.

Cranberry Spritzer: For a festive drink, thaw any unused portions of Iced Cranberry Sauce and mix with ginger ale or seltzer.

editor's favorite
BRIE BALLS WITH SPICY CRANBERRY DIPPING SAUCE

(photo on facing page)
Serve these Parmesan-crusted fried cheese balls right after frying so the centers are warm and oozy.

2   (8-ounce) rounds Brie
½   cup freshly grated Parmesan cheese
2   tablespoons chopped fresh parsley
1½ teaspoons minced garlic
4   large eggs, lightly beaten
1   cup all-purpose flour
1½ cups Italian-seasoned breadcrumbs
Vegetable oil
Spicy Cranberry Dipping Sauce

Trim rind from Brie. Combine Brie and next 3 ingredients in a large bowl; mix well with hands until combined. Shape cheese mixture into 1" balls. Dip balls in egg; dredge in flour. Dip again in egg; roll in breadcrumbs, pressing firmly so crumbs adhere. Place brie balls on wax paper; chill at least 1 hour.

Pour oil to a depth of 2" in a Dutch oven; heat to 370°. Fry cheese balls, in batches, until golden, about 1 minute; drain on paper towels. Serve immediately with Spicy Cranberry Dipping Sauce. Yield: 32 balls.

SPICY CRANBERRY DIPPING SAUCE
1   (16-ounce) can whole-berry cranberry sauce
1   tablespoon prepared horseradish
1   tablespoon orange juice

Combine all ingredients in a small bowl; stir well. Yield: 1¾ cups.

Broccoli Slaw with Cranberries

CRANBERRY AND APPLE RELISH

Spoon this tart relish over roast turkey or grilled pork tenderloin.

2   Granny Smith apples, chopped
4   teaspoons fresh lime juice
2   cups dried cranberries
3   green onions, sliced
2   jalapeño peppers, seeded and chopped
2   tablespoons honey
2   teaspoons apple cider vinegar

Combine apple and lime juice in a medium bowl, tossing well; drain.

Combine apples, cranberries, and remaining ingredients in a food processor, and pulse 6 to 8 times or until finely chopped. Cover and chill at least 1 hour. Yield: 4½ cups.

CRANBERRY-RASPBERRY CONSERVE

Hazelnuts are a flavor surprise in this gift-worthy topping.

1   (10-ounce) package frozen raspberries in syrup, thawed and undrained
2   cups fresh cranberries
1¾ cups sugar
½   cup golden raisins
½   cup finely chopped hazelnuts
1½ tablespoons grated orange rind

Process thawed raspberries in a blender or food processor 10 seconds or until pureed, stopping to scrape down sides. Pour berries through a wire-mesh strainer into a medium saucepan; press with the back of a spoon against sides of strainer to squeeze out juice, discarding solids.

Stir in cranberries; bring to a boil. Cover, reduce heat, and simmer 6 minutes or until skins pop.

Stir in sugar and remaining ingredients; bring to a boil. Cover, reduce heat, and simmer 2 minutes or until thickened, stirring constantly. Remove from heat. Spoon conserve into 3 (½-pint) jars, filling to ¼" from top. Cover with metal lids, and screw on bands. Store in refrigerator. Yield: 3 half-pints.

BROCCOLI SLAW WITH CRANBERRIES

Serve this pretty slaw as a side dish for turkey or ham or with a turkey sandwich or rollup.

½   cup apple cider vinegar
¾   cup sugar
½   teaspoon salt
½   teaspoon mustard seeds
3   tablespoons vegetable oil
1   (12- or 16-ounce) package broccoli slaw mix
2   Gala apples, chopped
1   cup dried cranberries

Combine first 4 ingredients in a small saucepan. Bring to a boil; boil 1 minute or until sugar dissolves. Remove from heat, and cool; whisk in oil. Combine slaw mix, apples, and cranberries in a large bowl. Pour vinaigrette over broccoli slaw, and toss well. Cover and chill. Serve with a slotted spoon. Yield: 8 cups.

Cranberry and Apple Relish over grilled pork tenderloin

Mesclun Salad with
Cranberries and
Avocado

❄*editor's favorite • quick & easy*

MESCLUN SALAD WITH CRANBERRIES AND AVOCADO

2   (5-ounce) bags gourmet mixed salad greens with herbs (we tested with Dole)
2   ripe avocados, coarsely chopped
1   cup walnut halves, toasted
¾   cup dried cranberries
½   cup blush wine vinaigrette (we tested with Briannas)
¼   teaspoon freshly ground pepper

Toss salad greens, avocado, walnuts, and cranberries in a serving bowl. Lightly dress salad with desired amount of vinaigrette; toss gently to coat. Sprinkle with pepper; toss again before serving. Yield: 6 servings.

CRANBERRY WALDORF SALAD

This tangy, lightly dressed salad is a great accompaniment with a casual holiday meal.

¼   cup sour cream
2   tablespoons mayonnaise
1½   tablespoons sugar
¼   teaspoon grated lime rind
1½   tablespoons lime juice (about 2 limes)
3   medium Granny Smith apples, chopped
1   ripe red pear, chopped
1   cup sweetened dried cranberries (we tested with Craisins)
1½   cups coarsely chopped pecans or walnuts, toasted
1½   cups chopped celery
1   cup miniature marshmallows

Whisk together first 5 ingredients in a large bowl. Add apple and next 4 ingredients to sour cream mixture; toss well. Cover and chill salad at least 1 hour. Stir in marshmallows just before serving. Yield: 4 to 6 servings.

CRANBERRY MINI MUFFINS

These petite not-so-sweet muffins are perfect for Christmas morning. Leftovers freeze well for up to a month.

2   cups self-rising flour
1   (8-ounce) container sour cream
1   cup butter, melted
1   teaspoon grated orange rind
1   tablespoon orange juice
1   (5-ounce) package sweetened dried cranberries (we tested with Craisins)
¼   cup sugar
¼   teaspoon ground cinnamon

Combine first 5 ingredients in a large bowl; stir well. Stir in cranberries.

Spoon batter into lightly greased miniature (1¾") muffin pans, filling full.

Combine sugar and cinnamon; sprinkle on muffins.

Bake at 400° for 19 to 20 minutes or until golden. Serve warm. Yield: 32 muffins.

CRANBERRY ICE

Here's a very easy, sweet, and light make-ahead dessert. Serve shavings of the rosy combo in stemmed glasses.

2   cups water
1   cup sugar
2½   cups cranberry juice cocktail or cranberry-apple juice drink

Stir together water and sugar in a saucepan. Bring to a boil, stirring until sugar dissolves. Remove from heat. Cool.

Stir in cranberry juice. Pour mixture into an 8" square pan. Cover and freeze 4 hours or until frozen. Remove from freezer; let stand 10 to 15 minutes. Shave ice by scraping with a fork. Scoop ice into glasses, and serve immediately, or store in an airtight container in freezer until ready to serve. Yield: 7 cups.

Cranberry Ice

THE DESSERTS

Mom's Pecan Pie

editor's favorite • make ahead

MOM'S PECAN PIE

We liked the double thick crust on this classic Southern pie. Substitute chopped pecans, a less expensive choice, for pecan halves, if desired.

1 (15-ounce) package refrigerated piecrusts
3 large eggs
1 cup sugar
¾ cup light corn syrup
2 tablespoons butter or margarine, melted
2 teaspoons vanilla extract
¼ teaspoon salt
1½ cups pecan halves

Unfold and stack 2 piecrusts; gently roll or press together. Fit into a 9" pieplate according to package directions; fold edges under, and crimp.

Stir together eggs and next 5 ingredients; stir in pecans.

Pour filling into piecrust. Bake at 350° for 50 to 55 minutes or until set. Serve warm, or cool completely on a wire rack. Yield: 1 (9") pie.

editor's favorite • make ahead

PUMPKIN PIE WITH MAPLE CREAM AND SUGARED PECANS

1⅓ cups all-purpose flour
½ teaspoon salt
½ cup shortening
4 to 5 tablespoons ice water
2 cups canned pumpkin
⅔ cup firmly packed light brown sugar
¼ cup granulated sugar
1 teaspoon ground cinnamon
½ teaspoon ground ginger
¼ teaspoon salt
¼ teaspoon ground allspice
¼ teaspoon ground nutmeg
1½ teaspoons grated orange rind
1½ cups half-and-half
3 large eggs, beaten
2 tablespoons granulated sugar
½ cup chopped pecans
1 cup whipping cream
¼ cup powdered sugar
¼ cup maple syrup

Combine flour and ½ teaspoon salt; cut in shortening with a pastry blender until mixture resembles the size of peas. Sprinkle ice water, 1 tablespoon at a time, evenly over surface; stir with a fork until dry ingredients are moistened. Shape dough into a ball; cover and chill 30 minutes.

Roll dough to ⅛" thickness on a lightly floured surface. Fit into a 9" deep-dish pieplate; trim off excess pastry along edges. Fold edges under, and crimp. Line pastry with aluminum foil, and fill with pie weights or dried beans. Bake at 450° for 8 minutes. Remove weights and foil; bake pastry 4 more minutes. Remove pastry crust to a wire rack to cool; reduce oven temperature to 375°.

Whisk together pumpkin and next 10 ingredients in a large bowl until combined. Pour filling into crust.

Bake at 375° for 50 to 55 minutes or until a knife inserted near center comes out clean, shielding crust after 20 minutes. Cool on a wire rack. Cover and refrigerate overnight.

Combine 2 tablespoons granulated sugar and pecans in a small skillet. Cook over medium-low heat, stirring constantly, 5 minutes or until sugar melts and pecans are toasted. Spoon onto wax paper to cool. Crumble sugared pecans into pieces.

Beat whipping cream at high speed with an electric mixer until foamy; gradually add powdered sugar, 1 tablespoon at a time, until soft peaks form. Slowly fold maple syrup into whipped cream. Cover and chill 1 hour.

To serve, spoon maple cream onto each serving. Sprinkle sugared pecans over cream. Yield: 1 (9") deep-dish pie.

Butternut Squash Pie: You can make this pie using butternut squash in place of the pumpkin. Two cups pureed butternut squash is about 1 (2-pound) squash.

Pumpkin Pie with Maple Cream and Sugared Pecans

editor's favorite
TRIPLE NUT CRANBERRY-APPLE CRISP

A chunky, nutty streusel meets tart apple filling in this fruit crisp. The key to the streusel topping is pinching large lumps together with your fingers.

1½ cups all-purpose flour
½   cup firmly packed light brown sugar
½   teaspoon ground cinnamon
¼   teaspoon salt
¼   teaspoon ground nutmeg
¾   cup cold butter, cut into pieces
½   cup coarsely chopped pecans
½   cup slivered almonds
½   cup coarsely chopped walnuts
8   Granny Smith apples, peeled, cored, and sliced (about 9 cups)
1   (12-ounce) container cranberry-orange crushed fruit (we tested with Ocean Spray)
½   cup granulated sugar
2   tablespoons all-purpose flour
1   teaspoon vanilla extract
½   teaspoon ground cinnamon
Vanilla ice cream or lightly sweetened whipped cream (optional)

Combine first 5 ingredients in a medium bowl. Cut in butter with a pastry blender until mixture is the size of peas. Stir in pecans, almonds, and walnuts; pinch mixture with fingers to form large lumps of streusel.

Stir together apple and next 5 ingredients. Spoon filling into a greased 13" x 9" baking dish. Sprinkle streusel topping evenly over filling.

Bake, uncovered, at 350° for 1 hour or until apples are tender and topping is golden. Remove from oven; let stand 10 to 15 minutes. Serve with vanilla ice cream or lightly sweetened whipped cream, if desired. Yield: 8 to 10 servings.

editor's favorite
BROWN SUGAR MERINGUE PIE

Here's a mile-high showstopper meringue dessert. Pies like this are meant to be served the day they're made.

1   cup firmly packed light brown sugar
⅓   cup cornstarch
⅛   teaspoon salt
2   cups half-and-half
4   egg yolks
2   teaspoons vanilla extract
¼   cup butter, cut into pieces
¾   cup firmly packed light brown sugar
⅔   cup granulated sugar
6   tablespoons water
5   egg whites
½   teaspoon cream of tartar
1   baked 9" pastry shell

Combine first 3 ingredients in a 4-quart heavy saucepan. Stir in half and-half. Cook, stirring constantly, over medium heat 9 minutes or until mixture comes to a boil and thickens. Boil 2 minutes, stirring constantly. Remove from heat.

Lightly beat egg yolks with a wire whisk. Gradually stir about one-fourth of hot mixture into yolks; add to remaining hot mixture, stirring constantly. Cook, stirring constantly, 3 minutes over medium heat. Remove from heat, and stir in vanilla and butter. Cover and set aside while preparing meringue.

Stir together ¾ cup brown sugar, ⅔ cup granulated sugar, and water in a 1-quart heavy saucepan. Bring to a boil over medium heat, stirring constantly, until sugar dissolves. Wash down crystals with a small pastry brush dipped in hot water. Bring to a boil over medium heat, and cook, stirring often, until a candy thermometer registers 246° (firm ball stage).

▲▲

. . . brown sugar meringue pie pointers . . .

For best results, time the beating of the egg whites as close as possible to the readiness of the syrup. Since this meringue is baked for only 9 minutes, it's essential that the syrup be at 246° when added to the egg whites to bring them to a safe temperature.

Be sure to use a heavy-duty stand mixer with at least a 4-quart bowl to accommodate the large volume of meringue. Don't be tempted to spread on all the meringue at once. It's necessary to apply it in 3 batches in order to fit it all on the pie and ensure maximum volume.

▼▼▼▼▼▼▼▼▼▼▼▼▼▼▼▼▼▼▼▼▼▼▼▼▼▼▼▼▼▼▼▼▼▼▼▼▼▼

While syrup cooks, beat egg whites and cream of tartar in a large bowl at high speed with a heavy-duty stand mixer until soft peaks form. Pour hot syrup mixture in a heavy stream over beaten egg whites, beating constantly at high speed until stiff peaks form (about 2 to 3 minutes). (Do not overbeat.)

Pour hot filling into pastry shell. Spoon one-third of meringue over hot filling in about 5 large dollops. Using back of a large spoon, spread meringue, sealing to edge of pastry and forming decorative swirls. Spread another third of meringue over pie, using same procedure. Spread remaining third of meringue over pie, and spread to edge.

Bake at 375° for 9 minutes or until meringue is lightly browned. Let cool completely on a wire rack. Yield: 1 (9") pie.

CRANBERRY MERINGUE PIE

Cranberry Meringue Pie

½ (15-ounce) package refrigerated piecrusts
2 (12-ounce) packages fresh or frozen cranberries
1 cup sugar
⅓ cup cranberry-apple juice drink
⅛ teaspoon salt
3 tablespoons cornstarch
⅓ cup water
1 teaspoon grated fresh ginger
2 tablespoons butter
1 teaspoon vanilla extract
3 egg whites
½ teaspoon cream of tartar
⅓ cup sugar
½ teaspoon grated lime rind

Fit piecrust into a 9" pieplate according to package directions; fold edges under, and crimp. Prick crust.

Bake at 450° for 8 minutes or until golden. Remove from oven, and cool completely. Reduce oven temperature to 325°.

Combine cranberries, 1 cup sugar, cranberry-apple juice drink, and salt in a large saucepan. Bring to a boil; reduce heat, and simmer, uncovered, over medium heat, stirring often, 5 to 7 minutes or until cranberry skins pop. Pour cranberries through a wire-mesh strainer into a bowl; discard solids.

Return cranberry mixture to saucepan. Combine cornstarch and water; stir into cranberry mixture. Add ginger. Bring to a boil over medium-high heat, and cook 1 minute, stirring constantly. Remove from heat; stir in butter and vanilla.

Beat egg whites and cream of tartar at high speed with an electric mixer until foamy. Add ⅓ cup sugar, 1 tablespoon at a time, beating until stiff peaks form and sugar dissolves (2 to 4 minutes). Add lime rind, beating just until blended.

Pour hot cranberry filling into prepared crust. Spread meringue over hot filling, sealing to edge of pastry.

Bake at 325° for 25 to 27 minutes or until meringue is golden. Cool completely on a wire rack. Yield: 1 (9") pie.

Chocolate-Raspberry Truffle Cake

make ahead
CHOCOLATE-RASPBERRY TRUFFLE CAKE

1   (10-ounce) package frozen raspberries, thawed
⅓   cup water
⅓   cup sugar
½   cup unsalted butter, cut into pieces
12 ounces bittersweet chocolate, coarsely chopped
6   large eggs
2   tablespoons all-purpose flour
⅛   teaspoon almond extract
Sweetened whipped cream
Fresh berries (optional)

Puree raspberries in a food processor. Press raspberry mixture through a wire-mesh sieve, using the back of a spoon to squeeze out juice. Discard seeds. Bring juice to a boil over high heat; cook over medium heat, stirring often, until mixture is reduced to ½ cup. Remove from heat, and cool completely.

Butter an 8" round cakepan, and line bottom with wax paper.

Cook water and sugar in a saucepan over medium heat until sugar dissolves, stirring occasionally. Add butter, and cook, stirring occasionally, until butter melts. Remove from heat, and add chocolate; stir until smooth. Cool.

Whisk together raspberry reduction, eggs, flour, and almond extract in a large bowl. Add chocolate mixture, and beat at medium speed with an electric mixer until blended. Pour into prepared cakepan.

Place cakepan in a larger pan; add hot water to large pan to a depth of 1". Bake at 325° for 42 to 45 minutes. Remove from water bath. Cool cake completely in pan on a wire rack.

Run a thin knife around pan to loosen cake. Invert cake onto a platter; remove wax paper, and invert onto another platter.

Cut cake into wedges, and serve with sweetened whipped cream and fresh berries, if desired. Yield: 8 servings.

Make-Ahead Plan: If desired, cake can be made a day ahead. Cover and chill in refrigerator; let stand at room temperature at least 1 hour before serving.

GINGERBREAD SKILLET CAKE WITH PEARS

Serve this holiday-inspired cake as a dessert or as an interesting brunch dish in place of French toast or crêpes.

4   large Bosc pears, cored and sliced ¼" thick
2   tablespoons all-purpose flour
3   tablespoons unsalted butter
⅓   cup firmly packed light brown sugar
1   cup all-purpose flour
¼   cup granulated sugar
1   teaspoon baking powder
½   teaspoon baking soda
½   teaspoon salt
½   teaspoon ground cinnamon
½   teaspoon ground ginger
5   tablespoons unsalted butter, cut into pieces
⅓   cup buttermilk
¼   cup molasses

Toss together pears and 2 tablespoons flour. Set aside.

Melt 3 tablespoons butter in a 9" cast-iron skillet over medium heat. Sprinkle brown sugar evenly in skillet. Fan pear slices in skillet over brown sugar.

Combine 1 cup flour and next 6 ingredients in a large bowl. Cut 5 tablespoons butter into flour mixture with a pastry blender until crumbly. Add buttermilk and molasses, stirring just until moistened. Spread batter evenly over pears, leaving a 1" edge.

Bake at 350° for 45 minutes or until bubbly and browned. Cool in pan on a wire rack 30 minutes before serving. Serve warm with vanilla ice cream. Yield: 8 servings.

MARBLED BITTERSWEET CHOCOLATE-COFFEE CHEESECAKE

2   cups coffee and cream-filled chocolate sandwich cookie crumbs, about 20 cookies (we tested with Oreos)
2   tablespoons butter or margarine, melted
4   (8-ounce) packages cream cheese, softened
1½ cups sugar
4   large eggs
2   tablespoons instant coffee granules
3   tablespoons coffee liqueur
1   teaspoon vanilla extract
4   (1-ounce) bittersweet chocolate baking squares, melted and cooled

Stir together cookie crumbs and butter; press firmly into bottom of a 10" springform pan.

Bake at 325° for 12 minutes. Cool on a wire rack.

Meanwhile, beat cream cheese at medium speed with an electric mixer until creamy; gradually add sugar, beating well. Add eggs, 1 at a time, beating until blended after each addition. Stir coffee, liqueur, and vanilla into batter.

Reserve 2½ cups batter; pour remaining batter into crust.

Stir melted chocolate into reserved batter. Spoon dollops of chocolate batter over coffee batter. Swirl batter gently with a knife.

Place springform pan in a large round shallow pan, and add hot water to shallow pan to a depth of 2".

Bake at 325° for 55 minutes or until cheesecake is almost set. Turn off oven, and let cheesecake stand in closed oven 30 minutes. Remove from oven; gently run a knife around edges to loosen sides. Cool on a wire rack; cover and chill 8 hours. Yield: 10 to 12 servings.

RED VELVET CUPCAKES

Tender little cakes are lathered with buttery cream cheese icing and snowy coconut.

1½ cups sugar
2   cups vegetable oil
2   large eggs
2   (1-ounce) bottles red liquid food coloring
1   teaspoon white vinegar
2½ cups all-purpose flour
2   tablespoons unsweetened cocoa
1   teaspoon baking soda
1   teaspoon salt
1   cup buttermilk
1   teaspoon vanilla extract
Cream Cheese Frosting
Sweetened flaked coconut (optional)

Beat sugar and oil at medium speed with an electric mixer until blended. Add eggs, 1 at a time, beating until blended after each addition. Add food coloring and vinegar, beating until blended.

Combine flour and next 3 ingredients; add to sugar mixture alternately with buttermilk, beginning and ending with flour mixture, beating just until blended. Stir in vanilla. Pour batter into muffin pans lined with paper liners, filling two-thirds full.

Bake at 350° for 18 minutes or until a wooden pick inserted in center comes out clean. Remove from pans, and cool completely on a wire rack. Spread generously with Cream Cheese Frosting. Sprinkle with coconut, if desired. Yield: 26 cupcakes.

CREAM CHEESE FROSTING
½   cup butter, softened
1   (8-ounce) package cream cheese, softened
1   (1-pound) package powdered sugar, sifted (4½ cups)
1   teaspoon vanilla extract

Beat butter and cream cheese at medium speed with an electric mixer until smooth. Gradually add powdered sugar, beating at low speed until light and fluffy. Stir in vanilla. Yield: 2¼ cups.

Red Velvet Cupcakes

Chocolate Meringue Cake

CHOCOLATE MERINGUE CAKE

This showstopper cake has several make-ahead steps to make your work easier than it looks. Give the extra meringues away in Christmas gift bags.

5   large eggs, separated
1   cup butter, softened
2   cups sugar
1   cup buttermilk
2   teaspoons vanilla extract
2¼ cups all-purpose flour
¼   cup Dutch-process cocoa
1   teaspoon baking soda
1   cup sweetened flaked coconut
⅔   cup finely chopped pecans
Cream Cheese Filling
Ganache
Meringues

Beat egg whites at high speed with an electric mixer until stiff peaks form; set aside.

Beat butter at medium speed until creamy; gradually add sugar, beating well. Add egg yolks, 1 at a time, beating until blended after each addition.

Combine buttermilk and vanilla. Combine flour, cocoa, and baking soda; add to butter mixture alternately with buttermilk mixture, beginning and ending with flour mixture. Beat at low speed until blended after each addition. Stir in coconut and pecans. Fold in beaten egg whites. Pour batter into 3 greased and floured 9" round cakepans.

Bake at 350° for 19 to 20 minutes or until a wooden pick inserted in center comes out clean. Cool in pans 10 minutes. Remove cake layers to wire racks, and cool completely.

Spread Cream Cheese Filling between layers. Spread Ganache on top and sides of cake, reserving ½ cup ganache. Mound Meringues on top of cake. Drizzle meringues with reserved ganache. To serve cake, remove meringues with small tongs, and serve a few meringues as a garnish with each serving. Yield: 1 (3-layer) cake.

8" Cake Variation: For 8" cake layers, bake layers 22 minutes or until a wooden pick inserted in center comes out clean.

Storage Tip: Refrigerate leftover cake without meringues. Store meringues in an airtight container at room temperature.

CREAM CHEESE FILLING
2   (3-ounce) packages cream cheese, softened
½   cup butter, softened
½   teaspoon vanilla extract
½   teaspoon almond extract
2¾ cups sifted powdered sugar

Beat first 4 ingredients at medium speed with an electric mixer until smooth. Gradually add powdered sugar, beating until light and fluffy. Yield: 2½ cups.

GANACHE
¾   cup whipping cream
6   (4-ounce) packages semisweet chocolate baking bars, finely chopped (we tested with Ghirardelli)

Bring whipping cream to a simmer in a heavy saucepan over medium heat. Remove from heat; add chocolate, stirring until melted. Cool until spreading consistency, stirring often. Yield: 2½ cups.

MERINGUES
2   egg whites
1½ teaspoons white vinegar
⅛   teaspoon salt
½   cup sugar
1   (4-ounce) package semisweet chocolate baking bar, finely chopped (we tested with Ghirardelli)

Beat egg whites, vinegar, and salt at high speed with an electric mixer until foamy; gradually add sugar, beating until stiff peaks form and sugar dissolves. Fold in chocolate. Drop by heaping teaspoonfuls onto parchment paper-lined baking sheets. Bake at 250° for 35 minutes. Transfer to wire racks to cool completely. Yield: 3 dozen.

Make-Ahead Elements: Bake cake layers ahead, and freeze up to 1 month. Bake meringues a day ahead, and store in tins. Prepare Cream Cheese Filling a day ahead, and store in refrigerator. Thaw cake layers at room temperature before assembling cake.

Coffee Jelly

make ahead
COFFEE JELLY

Try your favorite flavored coffee in this old-fashioned dessert. Decorate each dessert plate with melted vanilla ice cream and chocolate sauce.

2   envelopes unflavored gelatin
¾   cup Kahlúa
3   cups hot brewed coffee
¾   cup sugar
Pinch of salt
1   cup whipping cream, whipped
Chocolate shavings

Sprinkle gelatin over Kahlúa in a small bowl; let stand 5 minutes to soften gelatin. Add hot coffee, sugar, and salt; stir until gelatin dissolves (about 2 minutes).

Pour into 6 or 8 lightly greased 4" (½ cup) brioche molds; cover and chill overnight.

Use fingers to gently pull jelly away from edges of each mold; unmold onto dessert plates. Dollop with whipped cream; sprinkle with chocolate shavings. Yield: 6 to 8 servings.

Unmolding Tip: If jelly does not unmold easily, very quickly dip bottom of each mold into hot water to loosen; unmold onto dessert plates.

JAM PIE

This pie offers flexibility by using any jam that fits your taste. Choose your favorite jam that will complement the almond flavor in this dessert.

½   cup butter or margarine
3   egg yolks
1   large egg
½   cup sugar
¼   cup almond paste, crumbled
½   (15-ounce) package refrigerated piecrusts
⅓   cup seedless raspberry or blackberry jam
Powdered sugar (optional)

Melt butter, and let cool.

Beat egg yolks and egg at medium speed with an electric mixer until thickened. Add sugar and almond paste,

and beat well. (Filling will be slightly lumpy.) Add cooled butter, beating just until blended.

Fit piecrust into a 9" pieplate according to package directions; fold edges under, and crimp.

Stir jam well, and spread in bottom of pastry. Stir filling, and pour over jam.

Bake at 325° for 45 minutes or until set and a golden crust has formed on top, shielding edges with aluminum foil after 30 minutes to prevent excessive browning. Cool completely on a wire rack. Serve at room temperature. Dust with powdered sugar before serving, if desired. Store in refrigerator. Yield: 1 (9") pie.

editor's favorite • make ahead
CHOCOLATE TOFFEE BAR CAKE

Here's an easy out for a homemade holiday dessert. It gets really moist the second day.

1   (18.25-ounce) package German chocolate cake mix (we tested with Duncan Hines)
1   (14-ounce) can sweetened condensed milk
1   (12.25-ounce) jar caramel topping
1   (8-ounce) container frozen whipped topping, thawed
3   (1.4-ounce) English toffee candy bars, crushed (we tested with Skor bars)

Prepare cake according to package directions in a greased 13" x 9" pan. Cool completely in pan on a wire rack.

Gently poke holes in top of cake, using the end of a wooden spoon (wipe spoon clean after each hole). Combine sweetened condensed milk and caramel topping in a small bowl; slowly pour over cake. Spread whipped topping over cake. Sprinkle with crushed candy. Cover and chill until ready to serve. Yield: 12 servings.

Food Gifts & Wrapping Ideas

*How fun it is to give during this joyful
season of goodwill! The following pages offer nine
delicious recipes complete with packaging ideas that are
designed to be delightful. We also show easy ways
to trim presents for extra-special impact.*

Small Packages

Coffee-Pecan
Fudge ✳

COFFEE-PECAN FUDGE

For gift giving, we poured this dark chocolate fudge into mini loafpans, then sliced each loaf and individually wrapped each rich, thick slice.

2   cups sugar
½   cup butter, cut into pieces
2   tablespoons instant coffee granules
⅛   teaspoon salt
1   (5-ounce) can evaporated milk
12   large marshmallows
1   cup semisweet chocolate morsels
1   cup chopped pecans, toasted
1   teaspoon vanilla extract

Combine first 6 ingredients in a 4-quart heavy saucepan. Cook over medium heat, stirring constantly, 10 to 15 minutes or until sugar dissolves and marshmallows melt. Bring to a boil. Cook, without stirring, until a candy thermometer registers 234° (soft ball stage). Remove from heat.

Stir in chocolate morsels until melted. Stir in pecans and vanilla. Spread fudge immediately into 2 aluminum foil-lined, buttered 5¾" x 3½" mini loafpans. Cool completely. Remove fudge from pans. Slice fudge into ½" slabs. Yield: 1⅓ pounds.

Note: Lining the loafpans with aluminum foil and buttering them makes it easy to remove uncut fudge from the pans in one piece to slice it.

Coffee-Pecan Fudge

Key Lime Fudge

KEY LIME FUDGE

In the candy category, this fudge tops our list.

1   (5-ounce) can evaporated milk
1⅔   cups sugar
½   teaspoon salt
12   large marshmallows
2   cups white chocolate morsels (we tested with Nestlé)
¼   cup grated lime rind (about 4 limes)
2   tablespoons Key lime juice

Line an 8" x 8" square pan with aluminum foil; grease foil with butter.

Combine first 3 ingredients in a large heavy saucepan over medium heat. Bring to a boil; boil 8 minutes, stirring constantly. Remove from heat. Add marshmallows and remaining 3 ingredients to milk mixture; stir until marshmallows and morsels are melted and mixture is smooth. Pour fudge into prepared pan. Cool completely. Cut into 1" squares. Yield: about 1 pound.

Note: If you can't find Key lime juice, use the same amount of fresh squeezed lime juice. The fudge will be slightly sweeter and less tart.

Cracker Candy

CRACKER CANDY

Adults will want this treat for themselves, so you may want to make two batches if children are around. Package this candy in tissue paper-lined gift bags with holiday trim.

2   sleeves round buttery crackers (76 crackers), broken in half
¾   cup butter
¾   cup firmly packed light brown sugar
2   cups milk chocolate morsels
¾   cup toasted chopped pecans
½   cup chopped white chocolate

Place crackers on a lightly greased aluminum foil-lined jellyroll pan.

Bring butter and brown sugar to a boil in a saucepan, stirring constantly; cook 3 minutes, stirring often. Pour mixture over crackers.

Bake at 350° for 5 minutes. Turn oven off. Sprinkle crackers with chocolate morsels. Let stand in oven 3 minutes or until chocolate melts. Spread melted chocolate evenly over crackers. Top with pecans and white chocolate. Cool completely, and break candy into pieces. Store in refrigerator. Yield: about 2 pounds.

HAZELNUT CRINKLE COOKIES

Chopped hazelnuts can be found on the baking aisle with other nuts. They come in a 2.25-ounce package, which yields about ½ cup.

1¼ cups finely chopped hazelnuts (see Note)
1   (13-ounce) jar chocolate-hazelnut spread (we tested with Nutella)
¼   cup shortening
1⅓ cups granulated sugar
2   large eggs
1   teaspoon vanilla extract
3   cups all-purpose flour
2   teaspoons baking powder
½   teaspoon salt
⅓   cup milk
Sifted powdered sugar

Bake hazelnuts in a shallow pan at 350° for 4 to 5 minutes or until toasted. Set aside. Beat chocolate-hazelnut spread and shortening at medium speed with an electric

Hazelnut
Crinkle Cookies

mixer until blended. Gradually add 1⅓ cups granulated sugar, beating well. Add eggs and vanilla; beat until blended.

Combine flour, baking powder, and salt; add to chocolate-hazelnut mixture alternately with milk, beginning and ending with flour mixture. Stir in toasted hazelnuts.

Shape dough into 1" balls; roll in powdered sugar. Place 2" apart on lightly greased baking sheets.

Bake at 375° for 8 to 10 minutes or until set. Remove to wire racks to cool. Yield: 7 dozen.

Note: If you're unable to find chopped hazelnuts, use whole nuts. Bake at 350° for 10 minutes or until skins pop. Rub with a kitchen towel until skins come off. Finely chop nuts.

make ahead
LITTLE LEMON-GINGER COOKIES

2½ cups all-purpose flour

1½ teaspoons baking soda

1   teaspoon ground ginger

1   teaspoon ground cinnamon

½   teaspoon salt

¼   teaspoon ground cloves

¾   cup butter, softened

1   cup firmly packed light brown sugar

1   large egg

2   tablespoons light molasses

3   tablespoons grated lemon rind

½   cup turbinado sugar

Combine first 6 ingredients in a large bowl; set aside.

Beat butter at medium speed with an electric mixer until creamy; gradually add 1 cup brown sugar, beating well. Add egg; beat until blended. Stir in molasses and lemon rind. Gradually stir in flour mixture until combined, stopping to scrape down sides. Cover and chill dough 2 hours.

Roll dough into ½" balls. Roll balls in turbinado sugar; place on a lightly greased baking sheet. Flatten to ¼" thickness with a flat-bottomed glass.

Bake at 375° for 7 minutes. Cool on baking sheet 1 minute. Remove to wire racks to cool completely. Yield: 9 dozen.

Cherry-and-Cream Baby Cakes

CHERRY-AND-CREAM BABY CAKES

These sweet little scones are the perfect size for popping into your mouth.

2   cups all-purpose flour

1   tablespoon baking powder

¼   teaspoon salt

½   cup sugar

⅓   cup cold butter, cut into pieces

¾   cup whipping cream

½   cup dried cherries, coarsely chopped

½   cup semisweet chocolate mini-morsels

¾   teaspoon almond extract

1   tablespoon whipping cream

2   tablespoons sugar

Combine first 4 ingredients in a bowl; cut butter into dry ingredients with a pastry blender until crumbly. Add ¾ cup whipping cream and next 3 ingredients, stirring with a fork until dry ingredients are moistened. Knead dough in bowl 2 or 3 times to incorporate dry ingredients.

Turn dough out onto a lightly floured surface; knead 3 or 4 times. Pat dough to ¾" thickness; cut with a lightly

Little Lemon-Ginger Cookies

JOY!

floured 1½" round cutter. Place scones on a lightly greased baking sheet. Chill 20 minutes. Brush scones with 1 tablespoon whipping cream, and sprinkle evenly with 2 tablespoons sugar.

Bake at 375° for 18 to 20 minutes or until scones are golden. Serve warm. Yield: 2 dozen.

❄make ahead
Cheesecake Cream Puffs

Here's an over-the-top bite-size dessert for serving company or gift giving.

Cheesecake Pastry Cream
1⅓ cups water
1   (11-ounce) package piecrust mix (we tested
      with Betty Crocker)
4   large eggs
Chocolate Ganache

Prepare Cheesecake Pastry Cream. Cover and chill.
Bring water to a boil in a medium saucepan. Add piecrust mix, stirring vigorously over medium-high heat until mixture leaves sides of pan and forms a smooth ball. Remove from heat, and cool 5 minutes.

Add eggs, 1 at a time, beating thoroughly with a wooden spoon after each addition; then beat until dough is smooth. Drop dough by heaping teaspoonfuls onto ungreased baking sheets.

Bake at 425° for 20 minutes or until golden and puffed; cool completely on a wire rack.

Pipe Cheesecake Pastry Cream into cream puffs through side of each cream puff, using a pastry bag fitted with a round pastry tip. Dip half of each cream puff in warm Chocolate Ganache. Store cream puffs in refrigerator. Yield: 30 cream puffs.

Cheesecake Pastry Cream
1   large egg
1   egg yolk
¼   cup sugar
3   tablespoons cornstarch
1   cup half-and-half
½   (8-ounce) package cream cheese, softened
1   tablespoon butter, softened
1   teaspoon vanilla extract
1   teaspoon grated orange rind

Whisk first 4 ingredients in a heavy saucepan. Gradually add half-and-half. Bring to a boil over medium heat, whisking constantly. Cook 1 to 2 minutes or until thickened and bubbly. Remove from heat; whisk in cream cheese and remaining ingredients until smooth. Transfer to a small bowl; cover and chill at least 4 hours. (Cheesecake Pastry Cream will be thick.) Yield: 2 cups.

Chocolate Ganache
6   tablespoons whipping cream
2   cups semisweet chocolate morsels

Microwave cream in a small glass bowl at HIGH 1 minute. Add morsels, and microwave 1 more minute; stir until smooth. Yield: 2 cups.

Cheesecake Cream Puffs

LITTLE CHERRY POUND CAKES

Test Kitchens Staffer Kelley Wilton adapted her great-grandmother's delicious pound cake into petite individual loaves for gift giving.

1   (10-ounce) jar maraschino cherries
¾   cup butter, softened
¾   cup shortening
3   cups sugar
6   large eggs
3¼ cups all-purpose flour
⅛   teaspoon salt
1   cup milk
1   teaspoon almond extract
1   teaspoon vanilla extract
Cherry Glaze
Garnish: maraschino cherry halves

    Drain jar of cherries, discarding juice. Chop cherries, and set aside.

    Beat butter and shortening at medium speed with an electric mixer until creamy. Gradually add sugar, beating 1 minute. Add eggs, 1 at a time, beating just until yellow disappears.

    Combine flour and salt; gradually add to butter mixture alternately with milk, beginning and ending with flour mixture. Beat at low speed just until blended. Stir in flavorings and ½ cup chopped cherries.

    Spoon batter into 7 greased and floured 5¾" x 3" mini loafpans. (We recommend greasing your pans with shortening for best results.)

    Bake at 300° for 55 minutes or until a wooden pick inserted in center comes out almost clean. Cool in pans on wire racks 10 minutes; remove cakes from pans, and place on wire racks set over wax paper. Drizzle Cherry Glaze over slightly warm cakes. Garnish, if desired.

    Refrigerate cakes to let glaze harden before wrapping. Wrap cakes individually in cellophane for gift giving. Yield: 7 mini pound cakes.

Little Cherry Pound Cakes

CHERRY GLAZE

¼ cup butter, softened
1 (3-ounce) package cream cheese, softened
2 cups powdered sugar
3 tablespoons milk
1 teaspoon vanilla extract
¼ cup chopped cherries (remaining cherries from recipe on facing page)

Beat butter and cream cheese at medium speed until creamy. Gradually add powdered sugar and milk; beat until smooth. Stir in vanilla and cherries. Yield: about 2 cups.

CARAMEL GINGERBREADS

We gilded the lily by adding caramel icing to these yummy gingerbreads. You'll have some delectable icing leftover; spoon it over banana nut bread, muffins, or pound cake.

2¾ cups all-purpose flour
1 tablespoon ground ginger
1 teaspoon baking soda
¾ teaspoon salt
¾ teaspoon ground nutmeg
½ teaspoon ground cinnamon
1 cup light molasses
½ cup butter
½ cup firmly packed light brown sugar
¾ cup whole buttermilk
2 large eggs, lightly beaten
1 tablespoon vanilla extract
Caramel Icing
Coarsely chopped pecans, toasted (optional)

Combine first 6 ingredients in a large bowl; set aside.
Combine molasses, butter, and brown sugar in a saucepan. Cook over medium heat, stirring constantly, until butter melts and sugar dissolves. Set aside to cool. Add cooled molasses mixture to dry ingredients. Stir in buttermilk, eggs, and vanilla; stir just until batter is smooth.
Pour batter into 6 individual connected mini Bundt pans, well-greased with shortening, filling almost full.
Bake at 350° for 22 to 25 minutes or until a wooden pick inserted in center comes out clean. Cool in pans on a wire rack 15 minutes; remove carefully from pans, and cool completely on wire rack.

Caramel Gingerbreads

Drizzle icing over cakes set on wire rack. Sprinkle with chopped pecans, if desired. Let icing harden before wrapping cakes for gift giving. Yield: 6 gingerbreads.

CARAMEL ICING

2 cups sugar
1 cup butter
1 cup evaporated milk
1 teaspoon vanilla extract

Combine sugar, butter, and milk in a large saucepan; bring to a boil over medium heat. Cover and cook 2 to 3 minutes to wash down sugar crystals from sides of pan. Uncover and cook, stirring constantly, until a candy thermometer registers 234° (soft ball stage). Remove from heat, and add vanilla (do not stir). Let cool 10 minutes. Beat at medium speed with an electric mixer 6 to 7 minutes or until icing is spreading consistency. Yield: 2⅔ cups.

Note: Find mini Bundt pans at Williams-Sonoma or other cook stores.

SIMPLY BEAUTIFUL
GIFT WRAPS

*It's always exciting to get presents at Christmas,
but with these clever packaging ideas it's as much fun
to wrap as it is to receive.*

◀ PAPER CUTS

A rectangle of black cardstock sets the stage for a jaunty Christmas tree. The tree shown here consists of geometric shapes cut from handmade paper. The pieces are glued onto the rectangle, which is centered on the package. Also try white paper circles on a blue background to make a snowman.

GOODY BASKET ▲

If a gift is just too cute to close up in a box, present it in a basket instead. A small metal basket purchased for pennies at a yard sale is filled with shredded paper to show off its brightly colored treats. For a tag, cut a design from recycled cards or papers, and tie it on with a ribbon.

BEAD IT

Colorful bugle beads glued in the shapes of
letters make terrific package tags. For the tag,
cut a shape from cardstock, and make a hole
with a hole punch. Write the to/from information on the back of the tag, or leave space on
the front, if desired. Use this idea to create
Christmas cards, too. Fold a sheet of cardstock or other heavyweight paper in half, and
glue beads into holiday shapes or
messages on the front of the card.

BEJEWELED BOXES ▲

Give a regal air to packages with the simple addition of pendant-style ornaments. Tied onto a fluffy bow, these package toppers are a quick way to make a gift appear very special indeed. Old chandelier pendants give the same effect and can often be purchased inexpensively at flea markets or yard sales. For a snowy look, use clear pendants. A vivid color, such as the red pendant shown here against gold-and-white paper, gives a more dramatic impact.

◄ SWEET SCENTS

A lavender sachet is such a treat as a package topper—and it's so easy to do. To make the bag, fold a length of 2- to 3-inch-wide sheer ribbon in half. Stitch or glue the sides together. Tuck the unfinished top edges into the bag. Fill the bag with lavender, which can be purchased at crafts stores, and tie the top with a ribbon or silky cord.

NOT-SO-PLAIN BROWN PAPER BAG ▶

Who would guess that this classy wrap began as a basic paper lunch sack? To create the look shown here, glue a length of beaded trim (found at fabric or crafts stores) near the top of the sack. We curved ours slightly for a rounded edge; however, a straight line works just as well. Next, tear the edge of a piece of decorative paper to fit over the top of the front side of the bag, folding the top edge of the paper over the top of the bag. Be sure your paper collar covers the top of the glued-on trim. Use a hole punch to make two holes on each side of the bag. Thread a length of ribbon through the holes on each side, and knot the ends on the inside of the bag to make handles. The ribbon knots will also hold the paper collar in place. If desired, hang an ornament or gift tag from the trim.

EASY-WEAVE WRAPPINGS ▼

Make a few cuts in a box with a craft knife, weave through some pretty ribbon, and you'll wind up with a stunningly creative gift package. Pair solid-colored boxes with complementary ribbons, like the white box shown below, and you won't even need wrapping paper. Use the same idea for a package topper, and weave ribbon through paper that blends with the gift wrap.

COPYCAT CLASSICS

Here's a smart idea for wrapping small packages. Photocopy pieces of fabric from your scrap bag, and use the copies as wrapping paper. Bright red ribbons are the perfect match for the black-and-white papers, and they add just the right Christmassy accent.

◄ TAG IT WITH STYLE

When you start to wrap your Christmas gifts this year, bring out your favorite papers and ribbons, get the glue and scissors, and then engage your imagination. Think outside the red-and-green box. Use fresh combinations of colors and materials like the boxes shown here for gift packages that will really be noticed.

Make distinctive tags by cutting designs from wrapping paper or recycled cards and gluing them to solid-colored cardstock cutouts. To make them personal, cut interesting shapes from vellum and apply monograms using rub-on initials (find vellum paper and initials at crafts or office supply stores). Make holes with a hole punch.

MAGNETIC ATTRACTION ►

Tin containers make ideal gift boxes. They don't require wrapping, and they can be recycled for countless uses by the lucky recipient. Ribbons, paper cutouts, and, in this case, magnets, make this utilitarian piece a festive work of art. The beaded snowflake attached to a thin magnet was purchased at a crafts store and can be used on the fridge after the holiday. Also consider holiday motifs cut from old cards as decorative toppers for tins. A few drops of glue will hold them in place. Wrap the container with strips of ribbon, and add a tag to complete the package.

WHERE TO FIND IT

Source information is current at the time of publication; however, we cannot guarantee availability of items. If an item is not listed, its source is unknown.

page 9—Santa: Christmas & Co.; Birmingham, AL; (205) 943-0020; www.christmasandco.com

page 11—plates, copper pieces, santons: King's House Antiques; Mountain Brook, AL; (205) 871-5787

page 12—Santa, sleigh, candleholders, tray, mirror: King's House Antiques; Mountain Brook, AL; (205) 871-5787

page 13—reindeer: King's House Antiques; Mountain Brook, AL; (205) 871-5787

page 17—ornaments: Seasons of Cannon Falls™; www.seasonsofcannonfalls.com for a retailer near you

page 19—pitcher, plate: Two's Company; (914) 664-2277; www.twoscompany.com

pages 20–21—everything pictured: King's House Antiques; Mountain Brook, AL; (205) 871-5787

page 25—luminaire: *Southern Living At HOME®*; www.southernlivingathome.com for ordering information; **ornaments:** Henhouse Antiques; Birmingham, AL; (205) 918-0505

page 28—garland, greenery: Sugar Mountain Wreath & Garland; P.O. Box 788; Newland, NC; (800) 892-7440

page 32—tall lantern: *Southern Living At HOME®*; www.southernlivingathome.com for ordering information

page 34—dried florals: Harmony Landing; Homewood, AL; (205) 871-0585; harmonylanding@aol.com; **ribbon:** Midori, Inc.; (800) 659-3049; www.midoriribbon.com

pages 36–37—garland: Sugar Mountain Wreath & Garland; P.O. Box 788; Newland, NC; (800) 892-7440

page 38—candleholders, mirror: King's House Antiques; Mountain Brook, AL; (205) 871-5787

page 40—twig tree: Rosegate Designs; Birmingham, AL; (205) 321-1345

page 43—stockings: Holly Tree Inc.; Birmingham, AL; (205) 879-2625; **chandelier pendants:** Spectrum Home Furnishings, Inc.; (800) 668-3899; www.freedomcrystal.com

pages 44–45—stockings, Santas, stocking holders: Christmas & Co.; Birmingham, AL; (205) 943-0020; www.christmasandco.com; **twig trees:** Two's Company; (914) 664-2277; www.twoscompany.com; **pinecone candelabra:** Seasons of Cannon Falls™; www.seasonsofcannonfalls.com for a retailer near you

page 46—stockings: Target; www.target.com; **wise men, tall angel, barley twist candlesticks, luminaires:** *Southern Living At HOME®*; www.southernlivingathome.com for ordering information

pages 48–49—containers, reindeer moss: Smith & Hawken; (800) 981-9888; www.smithandhawken.com

page 52—wise men, ribbon: Christmas & Co.; Birmingham, AL; (205) 943-0020; www.christmasandco.com; **trees and candleholders:** Henhouse Antiques; Birmingham, AL; (205) 918-0505

page 53—word and rope garlands, silver tree: Christmas & Co.; Birmingham, AL; (205) 943-0020; www.christmasandco.com; **bead garland:** Seasons of Cannon Falls™; www.seasonsofcannonfalls.com for a retailer near you

page 54—stockings, stocking holders: Ballard Designs; (800) 367-2775; www.ballarddesigns.com; **brown transferware tureen:** Mulberry Heights; Birmingham, AL; (205) 972-1300; **candlesticks, iron arched piece:** The Cottage Shop; Homewood, AL; (205) 871-7463; **red star weather vane:** Attic Antiques; Birmingham, AL; (205) 991-6887

page 55—stockings: Target; www.target.com

pages 56–57—hurricanes: Pottery Barn; (888) 779-5176; www.potterybarn.com

page 58—mugs: The China Closet; Vestavia Hills, AL; (205) 822-6499; **tiered metal centerpiece:** Christine's; Mountain Brook, AL; (205) 871-8297

page 59—bowl, painting: King's House Antiques; Mountain Brook, AL; (205) 871-5787

pages 60–61—ribbon: Christmas & Co.; Birmingham, AL; (205) 943-0020; www.christmasandco.com; **lemon leaf garland:** Martin & Son Wholesale Florist; Birmingham, AL; (205) 251-7673

page 63—fruit ornaments: Christmas & Co.; Birmingham, AL; (205) 943-0020; www.christmasandco.com; and Smith & Hawken; (800) 981-9888; www.smithandhawken.com; **ribbon:** Midori, Inc.; (800) 659-3049; www.midoriribbon.com

page 65—epergne, candlesticks: King's House Antiques; Mountain Brook, AL; (205) 871-5787

pages 66–67—centerpiece container and stand, table, chairs, chandelier, bench: King's House Antiques; Mountain Brook, AL; (205) 871-5787; **napkins, plates, crystal, flatware, chargers:** Table Matters; Mountain Brook, AL; (205) 879-0125; www.table-matters.com

pages 68–69—lamp: Henhouse Antiques; Birmingham, AL; (205) 918-0505; **rooster centerpiece, polka-dot bowls, flatware:** *Southern Living At HOME®*; www.southernlivingathome.com for ordering information; **checked dinnerware, glassware:** Christine's; Mountain Brook, AL; (205) 871-8297; **red salad plates:** Lenox (Rustic Berry); www.lenox.com; **pine sideboard:** The Cottage Shop; Homewood, AL; (205) 871-7463

page 70—reindeer: Christmas & Co.; Birmingham, AL; (205) 943-0020; www.christmasandco.com;

candleholders, leaf and berry garland, table runner, stockings, ornaments on side table: Christmas & Co.; Birmingham, AL; (205) 943-0020; www.christmasandco.com; and Seasons of Cannon Falls™; www.seasonsofcannonfalls.com for a retailer near you;

pitcher, salt and pepper, bowls, plates, chargers: *Southern Living At HOME®*; www.southernlivingathome.com for ordering information

page 72—mug: Chaleur; www.chaleur.com; sheer bag: Morex; www.jkmribbon.com

page 73—corkscrew: Seasons of Cannon Falls™; www.seasonsofcannonfalls.com for a retailer near you

pages 74–76—stockings: Monograms Plus; Birmingham, AL; (205) 985-3188;

plates and mugs: Bromberg & Co.; (800) 633-4616; www.brombergs.com; and Present Tense; (800) 282-7117; www.presenttense.com for a retailer near you

page 80—plates, flatware, glassware, napkins: Table Matters; Mountain Brook, AL; (205) 879-0125; www.table-matters.com; glass candlesticks: Two's Company; (914) 664-2277; www.twoscompany.com; ornaments: Christmas & Co.; Birmingham, AL; (205) 943-0020; www.christmasandco.com; ribbon: Midori, Inc.; (800) 659-3049; www.midoriribbon.com

page 84—platter: Present Tense (800) 282-7117; www.presenttense.com for a retailer near you

page 85—dress-me-up plate: *Southern Living At HOME®*; www.southernlivingathome.com for ordering information

page 87—plate: Present Tense; (800) 282-7117; www.presenttense.com for a retailer near you

page 90—tiered server: Flora; Homewood, AL; (205) 871-4004

page 93—pedestal server: Flora; Homewood, AL; (205) 871-4004

page 94—mug: Vietri; Hillsborough, NC; (800) 277-5933; www.vietri.com;

plate: Villeroy & Boch; www.villeroy-boch.com

page 96—Cook Store of Mountain Brook; Mountain Brook, AL; (205) 879-5277

page 97—cranberry glass, beaded tree, ornament: Henhouse Antiques; Birmingham, AL; (205) 918-0505

page 99—carving set: Tricia's Treasures; Homewood, AL; (205) 871-9779

page 101—dessert plates: TAG; (773) 871-1300

page 102—dessert plates, tins: Seasons of Cannon Falls™; www.seasonsofcannonfalls.com for a retailer near you;

snowman ornament: Attic Antiques; Birmingham, AL; (205) 991-6887

page 105—pewter platter: MATCH; Jersey City, NJ; (201) 792-9444; www.match1995.com

pages 106, 109—candlesticks: Lamb's Ears Ltd.; Birmingham, AL; (205) 969-3138; and Cast Art; Birmingham, AL; (205) 324-3936

pages 106–109—plates: Villeroy & Boch (Festive Memories); www.villeroy-boch.com

pages 106, 110–111—platter: Villeroy & Boch; www.villeroy-boch.com

page 114—platter: Vietri; Hillsborough,

NC; (800) 277-5933; www.vietri.com

page 116—sleigh, plates, platter: Mariposa; (800) 788-1304; www.mariposa-gift.com for a retailer near you

page 120—small red bowls: Table Matters; Mountain Brook, AL; (205) 879-0125; www.table-matters.com

page 121—soufflé dish: Williams-Sonoma; (800) 541-2233; www.williams-sonoma.com

page 128—bowl: Present Tense; (800) 282-7117; www.presenttense.com for a retailer near you

page 129—white bowl: The China Closet; Vestavia Hills, AL; (205) 822-6499

page 131—ornaments: Christmas & Co.; Birmingham, AL; (205) 943-0020; www.christmasandco.com

page 134—plate: Lenox (Rustic Berry); www.lenox.com

page 137—platter: Pottery Barn; (888) 779-5176; www.potterybarn.com

page 138—bowl: Two's Company; (914) 664-2277; www.twoscompany.com; salt and pepper: Williams-Sonoma; (800) 541-2233; www.williams-sonoma.com

page 141—dessert plates: Villeroy & Boch (Festive Memories); www.villeroy-boch.com

page 148—dress-me-up plate and server: *Southern Living At HOME®*; www.southernlivingathome.com for ordering information;

red dinnerware: Lenox (Rustic Berry); www.lenox.com

page 165—chandelier pendants: Spectrum Home Furnishings, Inc.; (800) 668-3899; www.freedomcrystal.com; and Seasons of Cannon Falls™; www.seasonsofcannonfalls.com for a retailer near you

page 166–167—snow village, ornament: Seasons of Cannon Falls™; www.seasonsofcannonfalls.com for a retailer near you

page 168—toile fabric: Waverly; (800) 988-7775; www.waverly.com

page 169—wrapping paper: Midori, Inc.; (800) 659-3049; www.midoriribbon.com

RECIPE INDEX

GENERAL INDEX

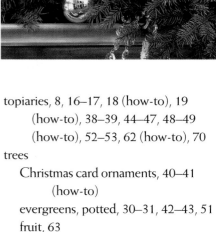

CONTRIBUTORS

EDITORIAL CONTRIBUTORS:

Rebecca Boggan   Rebecca Lang
Lauren Brooks   Maloy Love
Jennifer Cofield   Catherine Pewitt
Adrienne Davis   Frances Robinson
Connie Formby   Katie Stoddard
Caroline Grant   Carole Sullivan
Susan Huff   Amy Wilson
Shannon Jernigan   Jeannie Winford

THANKS TO THE FOLLOWING HOMEOWNERS:

Lisa Beasley   Beth and Jimmy Jordan
Lauren and Joel Brooks   Abby and Jeremiah Maddox
Kay and Eddie Clarke   Kristin and Bill Ritter
Carolyn and Joe Dorris   Katie and Tom Stoddard
Melanie and Jerry Grant   Sandra and Ben Zarzaur
Elizabeth and Tom Jernigan

THANKS TO THESE BIRMINGHAM BUSINESSES AND ORGANIZATIONS:

Bromberg & Company   King's House Antiques
Christine's   Lamb's Ears Ltd.
Christmas & Co.   Martin & Sons Wholesale Florist
The Cottage Shop   Monograms Plus
Davis Wholesale Florist   Table Matters
Flora   Tricia's Treasures
Henhouse Antiques

SPECIAL THANKS:

Seasons of Cannon Falls ™, Cannon Falls, Minnesota
Sugar Mountain Wreath & Garland, Newland, North Carolina

holiday
planning guide

Plan ahead, be prepared, and get off to a great start this holiday season. The following pages offer you the perfect way to stay organized. There are planning calendars, centerpiece ideas, cooking tips from our test kitchens, and gift-wrapping suggestions—not to mention lots of space to write notes, make lists, and be ready for all the fun the season has to offer.

NOVEMBER

Sunday	Monday	Tuesday	Wednesday
	1	2	3
7	8	9	10
14	15	16	17
21	22	23	24
28	29	30	

2004

Thursday	Friday	Saturday
4	5	6
11	12	13
18	19	20
Thanksgiving 25	26	27

ahead-of-the-game checklist

Stock up early on holiday necessities. Here's a list to help you keep track of the basics.

☐ Greeting cards
☐ Wrapping paper
☐ Gift bags
☐ Tissue paper
☐ Tape
☐ Gift tags
☐ Bows and ribbons
☐ Party invitations
☐ Stamps
☐ Seasonal fruits
☐ Cranberries
☐ Nuts
☐ Baking ingredients
☐ Extra napkins/table linens/dish towels
☐ Candles
☐ Fresh greenery clippings
☐ Wreaths and garlands
☐ Tree stand
☐ Holiday lights

things to do

DECEMBER

Sunday	Monday	Tuesday	Wednesday
			1
5	6	7	8
12	13	14	15
19	20	21	22
26	27	28	29

2004

Thursday	Friday	Saturday
2	3	4
9	10	11
16	17	18
23	Christmas Eve 24	Christmas 25
30	New Year's Eve 31	

party-ready cupboard

Here's a quick checklist of pantry staples to have on hand during the holidays.

- ☐ Coffee (both regular and flavored) and tea
- ☐ Wine and sodas
- ☐ Sweetened condensed milk
- ☐ Assorted nuts
- ☐ Semisweet morsels
- ☐ Baking chocolate
- ☐ Flaked coconut
- ☐ Frozen pie shells
- ☐ Canned broths
- ☐ Spices: ground allspice, cinnamon, cloves, ginger, and nutmeg
- ☐ Jams, jellies, preserves
- ☐ Eggnog
- ☐ Seasonal fresh herbs
- ☐ Cranberries
- ☐ Canned pumpkin
- ☐ Butter
- ☐ Frozen/refrigerated bread dough
- ☐ Whipping cream
- ☐ Hot chocolate

things to do

holiday countdown

There's so much to remember between Thanksgiving and Christmas. These reminders and planning tips will help.

IN NOVEMBER

• **Start baking holiday cookies and cakes.** You can freeze them (if they're unfrosted) for several months.

• **Purchase cranberries** while they're readily available at the local supermarket. They keep well in the freezer and come in handy for recipes and decorating.

• **Take stock of seasonal items,** such as holiday dinnerware and glasses, serving pieces, containers for arrangements, and Christmas decorations, to see what needs to be purchased or cleaned.

• **Update your Christmas card list,** and address envelopes.

• **Line up babysitters** for special events.

IN DECEMBER

• **Clip greenery for decorations.** To make the greenery stay fresh longer, immerse cut branches in water for 24 hours before adding to arrangements.

• **Stock the pantry** to avoid last-minute dashes to the grocery store for recipe ingredients (see page 181 for suggestions).

• **Put up wreaths and garlands midmonth.** Mist the greenery every few days to keep it green. For a special party, put fresh flowers in floral picks, and tuck them among the branches.

• **If ordering gifts by mail,** order the first week of December to ensure arrival by Christmas.

• **Mail Christmas cards** and packages early in the month.

DECORATING TO-DO LIST

Make dressing your home for the holidays a progressive event from Thanksgiving to Christmas. List your ideas here to get your imagination in gear.

Gather materials

from the yard:...

from around the house:...

from the store:...

Add holiday decorations

to the table:..

to the buffet:...

to the door:...

to the mantel:..

to the staircase:...

to the chandelier:..

other:...

mix-and-match holiday menus

These menu ideas are based on recipes in the book.

HOLIDAY BREAKFAST

Citrus Batida, page 97
Coffee
Scrambled eggs
Grits
Sweet Potato Hash Browns, page 127
Cranberry Mini Muffins, page 139

APPETIZER OPEN HOUSE

Poinsettia Punch, page 97
Wine
Herbed Nuts, page 91
Herb and Cheese Coins, page 91
Pesto Torte, page 97
Brie Balls with Spicy Cranberry Dipping Sauce,
page 135
Coffee-Pecan Fudge, page 155
White Chocolate-Thyme Truffles, page 94
Coffee   Hot cocoa

SANDWICH NIGHT

Turkey sandwiches with leftover turkey and
Cornbread Dressing Loaf, page 119
Cranberry-Orange Sauce, page 135
Parmesan-Rosemary Potatoes, page 125
Broccoli Slaw with Cranberries,
page 136

HOLIDAY DINNERS

Classic Roast Turkey and Gravy, page 111
Cranberry-Orange Sauce, page 135
Cornbread Dressing Croquettes, page 119
Sweet Potato Casserole, page 127
Peas with Browned Butter, Caramelized Onions, and Prosciutto,
page 130
Pumpkin Pie with Maple Cream and Sugared Pecans, page 141

Mesclun Salad with Cranberries and Avocado, page 138
Beef Tenderloin with Cranberry-Port Reduction and Gorgonzola
Butter, page 117
Garlic-Gruyère Mashed Potatoes, page 126
Roasted Broccoli with Buttered Walnuts, page 129
Chocolate-Raspberry Truffle Cake, page 145

Rosemary Roasted Turkey, page 95
Cranberry-Raspberry Conserve,
page 136
Fruited Wild Rice Dressing, page 122
Sweet Onion Pudding, page 100
Brussels sprouts
Mom's Pecan Pie, page 141

Roasted Turkey with White Wine-Sage Sauce,
page 112
Roasted Roots, page 133
Creamed Onion Gratin, page 130
Peas
Cranberry Ice, page 139

Hickory-Smoked Bourbon Turkey,
page 98
Green Chile-Cheddar-Pecan Dressing,
page 123
Honey-Glazed Cranberry Carrots, page 129
Cranberry and Apple Relish, page 136
Coffee Jelly, page 151

Pecan Chicken with Honey-Mustard Sauce,
page 117
Brussels Sprouts and Wild Rice, page 129
Green salad
Gingerbread Skillet Cake with Pears, page 145

Baked Burgundy Ham, page 115
Cider Mashed Sweet Potatoes, page 126
Green beans
Rosemary Buttermilk Biscuits, page 91
Mystery Pecan Pie, page 104

Minted Pork Loin, page 114
Homestyle Mashed Potatoes, page 125
Honey-Glazed Cranberry Carrots, page 129
Peas with Browned Butter, Caramelized
Onions, and Prosciutto, page 130

entertaining planner

Use these pages to write the important details that will help you stay on track with all your holiday party plans.

TREATS FOR INSTANT ENTERTAINING

Keep these items on hand for unexpected guests.

• **Keep ready-to-eat carrot and celery sticks in the refrigerator.** With a veggie dip or salad dressing, they make an easy snack or appetizer.
• **Set out cream cheese and preserves** as spreads for an assortment of crackers.
• **Bake muffins, and freeze them up to one month.** Reheat in the toaster oven or the microwave.
• **Store a container of cut-up brownies in the freezer.** For a quick dessert, pop brownies into the microwave, and then top with vanilla ice cream and hot fudge sauce.
• **Wrap a cheesecake in heavy-duty plastic wrap,** or place it in an airtight container; it will keep in the freezer up to one month. Freezing will not harm the flavor or texture. Thaw in the refrigerator. For an impressive topping, use a vegetable peeler to shave curls from the edges of a milk chocolate candy bar.

• **Brew coffee with strips of orange peel for added flavor.** Offer sugar cubes, whipped cream, and grated chocolate, along with cinnamon-stick stirrers.

TIME-SAVING MAKE-AHEADS

Save time in the kitchen with these suggestions.

• **When browning ground chuck,** brown extra to have on hand for quick meal preparation. It will keep in the freezer up to three months.
• **Chop green pepper or onion ahead of time for holiday cooking.** Freeze it in zip-top freezer bags up to three months.
• **Freeze extra sauce, gravy, or broth in ice-cube trays;** reheat the cubes as needed.
• **When you're shredding cheese for a recipe,** shred extra to freeze for later use.
• **Freeze leftover veggies** to be combined for soup later.

LAST-MINUTE DETAILS

Use this space as a final checklist before the party.

GUEST LIST

Use these lines to list names, addresses, and phone numbers of guests
you plan to invite to your holiday festivities.

....
....
....
....
....
....
....
....
....
....
....
....
....
....
....
....
....
....
....
....

PANTRY LIST

List an inventory of what you have and
what you need on these lines.

....
....
....
....
....
....
....
....
....
....
....
....

PARTY TO-DO LIST

Use this space to help jog your memory
as partytime approaches.

....
....
....
....
....
....
....
....
....
....
....
....

Christmas dinner planner

Here are some tips and tricks that will help as you plan the holiday feast.

TOP IDEAS FOR TERRIFIC TABLES

These centerpiece ideas are quick and easy, and many use items that you already have around the house.

• **Fill bowls with colorful ornaments,** and arrange them down the center of the table.

• **Cluster a collection of candles** in the center of the table for dramatic impact. Tuck in sprigs of greenery and berries among the candles.

• **To add height, light, and dimension to the table,** place pillar candles in clear glass vases, and fill in around the bottom of the candle with glass beads.

• **Add a charger plate to traditional china** for a festive update. Usually 12 inches in diameter, chargers are placed underneath dinner plates to create a framelike border around the plate. Gold or silver chargers blend with a variety of china patterns.

• **Pair inexpensive goblets painted with a Christmassy pattern** with white china for an easy holiday table setting.

• **Enhance a simple centerpiece** made of evergreen foliage by placing a mirror underneath. Arrange glittery ornaments at the base of the container.

• **Stack two glass cake stands,** and fill them with greenery and citrus fruit for a fresh and fragrant centerpiece. Add ribbon for a colorful accent.

GUEST LIST

Use these lines to list names, addresses, and phone numbers of guests you plan to invite to join you for Christmas dinner.

....

....

....

....

....

....

....

....

....

....

MENU IDEAS

....

....

....

....

....

....

TRIED-AND-TRUE TIPS FROM OUR TEST KITCHENS

These helpful hints from our experts take the guesswork out of holiday cooking.

• **When cooking with wine,** add it while the dish is still cooking briskly if you want the alcohol to have a chance to cook off.

• **When you whip heavy cream or egg whites,** use a large, deep bowl. The larger the bowl, the easier it is to incorporate air; plus, a deep bowl contains the mixture and prevents splattering. Also, make sure the bowl is free of all oil and fat residue; otherwise the cream or egg whites won't whip as high.

• **For best results, chop nuts by hand with a large, sharp knife.** If the nuts are to be used in baked goods, add a little flour or sugar from the list of ingredients to absorb any oil that's produced during processing. This will keep the nuts dry, which makes them spread more evenly throughout the batter or dough.

• **To toast small amounts of nuts,** place nuts in a dry skillet over medium heat for just a few minutes, stirring often. Use your sense of smell to judge when they're toasted, and watch them closely; the smaller the pieces, the quicker they cook.

• **When making cookies,** line baking sheets with parchment paper or special baking paper with a nonstick coating. The cookies won't stick, the liners minimize burning, and cleanup's a breeze.

• **To unmold a congealed salad,** begin by spraying the mold with cooking spray before filling. To unmold, run a spatula around the edges of the mold to let air underneath. Next, wet a dish towel with hot water, and wring out the excess. Wrap the towel around the bottom and sides of the mold, and let it stand 1 minute (not too long or the salad will start to melt). Invert a serving plate over the salad, and carefully flip the mold and plate over; then lift off the mold.

TURKEY TALK

If you roast a turkey only once or twice a year, these guidelines are good reminders of how to proceed.

• **To ready a whole turkey for cooking,** remove the giblets and neck, and rinse and cook them within 12 hours; they can be used to make gravy. Then rinse the turkey

inside and out, and pat dry. If you plan on stuffing the body cavity, do it just before roasting, never the night before. Lightly spoon stuffing into the body and neck cavities of the turkey, but don't pack it tightly because it needs room to expand during roasting. Also, remember that a cooked, stuffed turkey should never be refrigerated with the stuffing still inside; remove the stuffing, and refrigerate separately.

• **When stuffing food, especially poultry,** it's okay to prepare the stuffing mixture ahead, but don't add it to the bird until just before cooking. If stuffed in advance and allowed to stand, even if refrigerated, harmful bacteria may develop that may not be destroyed during cooking. And make sure the stuffing cooks to 165°; if the stuffing isn't done, and the bird is, then transfer the stuffing to a baking dish, and bake until it tests done. The easiest way to test the temperature is with an instant-read thermometer.

• **If all the stuffing doesn't fit in a turkey or chicken,** place the leftover stuffing in a casserole, and bake with the bird during the last 30 or 45 minutes of cooking.

DINNER TO-DO LIST

Write your list here to minimize last-minute surprises.

....
....
....
....
....
....
....
....
....
....
....
....
....
....
....
....
....
....
....

gifts and greetings
Use this page to make a list of everyone you want to include on your Christmas card and gift lists this year.

CHRISTMAS CARD INFO

• **Fine-tune your holiday card list** before you begin addressing envelopes.

• **Address the envelopes first.** Then write in the cards. This takes less time than looking up each name, one at a time.

• **Just address 5 to 10 cards a day** if your list seems overwhelming.

• **Put stamps and return address labels** on the envelopes while talking on the phone.

• **When you receive cards from other people,** immediately note any address changes on your list and in your address book.

MAILING INFO

• **Mail packages early in the day.** This helps relieve the afternoon crunch at the post office, and your items may be delivered a day earlier.

• **If using odd-sized cards** (such as square), note that extra postage may be required.

• **Box and send your addressed and stamped cards to the postmaster in one of these towns:**

Christmas, FL 32709
Santa Claus, IN 47579
Bethlehem, GA 30620
Mistletoe, KY 41351
Rudolph, OH 43462

The envelopes will be postmarked with the town's name on it.

CHRISTMAS CARD LIST

name	address	sent/received

GIFT LIST

PERFECT BOWS AS EASY AS 1-2-3

Here's the secret to a beautiful bow, in three quick steps.

1. Wrap a length of ribbon tightly around the package, and make a knot, leaving 2 inches of ribbon on each side.
2. With another ribbon, make a loop the desired size. Hold the ribbon with your fingers, and make the desired number of loops on either side of the center in the same manner.
3. Tie the center of the bow to the package, using the extra ribbon from the knot. Fluff and shape the bow.

EXTRAS:

• Layer narrow ribbons with wide ones for a pretty, multidimensional effect.
• Instead of ribbon, consider tying up packages with colored raffia, cording and tassels, or tulle.

BEYOND THE BOX

Instead of the basic paper box, consider these ideas for packaging gifts.

• Spray-painted coffee or chip cans (especially for food gifts)
• Produce baskets with holiday ribbons woven through the open spaces
• Decorative tins
• Plastic freezer bags (not zip-top) lined with tissue and tied with ribbons
• White bakery boxes tied with red and green ribbons or decorated with holiday stickers for a child's gift

holiday memories
Keep a reminder of this holiday's best moments by recording them on these pages.

TREASURED TRADITIONS
Whether it's a time-honored favorite or something new you'd like to try,
this is a good place to record it.

....
....
....
....
....
....
....
....
....
....
....
....
....
....
....
....
....

SPECIAL HOLIDAY EVENTS
List this season's most wonderful happenings on these lines. Make note
of a specific date if an event is something you'd like to do again next year.

....
....
....
....
....
....
....
....

HOLIDAY VISITS & VISITORS

Remember the highlights of all your
Christmas reunions by noting them here.

THIS YEAR'S FAVORITE RECIPES

Appetizers and Beverages..

....

....

....

....

....

Entrées...

....

....

....

....

....

Sides and Salads..

....

....

....

....

Cookies and Candies..

....

....

....

....

....

Desserts...

....

....

....

....

....

....

notes for next year

FAVORITE THINGS

Use this space to record the best-of-the-best. Whether it's parties, recipes, gift ideas, or impromptu gatherings, writing it here will ensure you'll remember it for the next holiday season.

GET A HEAD START

Plan now for a terrific Christmas 2005. With your best ideas written here, you'll be well on your way.